Killing It With

Direct Mail

For Real Estate Investors

If you are not using Direct Mail, you are leaving money on the table!

Jeff Charlton

Killing It With Direct Mail For Real Estate Investors
If you are not using Direct Mail,
you are leaving money on the table!

ISBN: 978-1-63110-396-4

Printed in the United States of America by
Graphic Connections Group
Chesterfield, Missouri 63005

Direct Mail is as powerful as ever,

and growing,

especially in the real estate field.

— — — — — — — — — — — — — —

Learn how to use direct mail marketing
to make more real estate deals than ever before.

Contents

Introduction

Real Estate Investing is tougher than ever in today's market. There are more and more competitors hitting the market every day. Because of this, you need all the help you can get to make sure that you are winning the battle in the marketplace. This book will help you do that.

My name is Jeff Charlton, and I own Graphic Connections Group. We specialize in creating, printing, and mailing effective direct mail campaigns for all types of industries. We pay special attention to real estate investors. We offer clients who understand the importance of direct mail marketing options that can increase the effectiveness, response rates, and ROI of their campaigns.

Our long term success is rooted in providing an over-the-top level of customer service – the kind you don't find very often in our world anymore.

Additionally, I have been a real estate investor for 30 years. Although I don't flip houses on a daily basis, I have done it in the past, and I do hold rental property right now. That's a benefit to you, because my team and I understand completely what it is you're looking for, and what you have to do to find and attract good leads.

This should matter to you because we really do care about your success. We will take the time to get to know who you are, and what you are trying to accomplish with your marketing dollars. We will work side-by-side with you to help create a program that exceeds your expectations.

This book will give you a basic education on why and how to use all sorts of direct mail pieces to effectively get your message out. The bottom line is we understand that you want to find and close deals. It's our job to help you find leads to do just that.

Before I get into the nitty-gritty details, let me just tell you briefly why I am uniquely qualified to educate you in the field of direct mail.

At the time of this writing, I am 56 years old. I have been a salesman and direct marketer since I was a Boy Scout at 11 years old. Yes that's right, 11. At that age, I was just a kid trying to sell fertilizer for my Boy Scout fundraiser. However, through the use of flyers that I dropped off at houses in my neighborhood, I was using direct response marketing.

I was self-employed at the age of 14 years old. I started painting houses during the summers and grew that business to a crew of 12 guys including my 4 football coaches by the time I was 18 years old and continued that business until I graduated from college with an engineering degree. I used direct mail marketing and door to door sales to sell painting jobs. I did spend a brief six year period after college working as an engineer for Proctor & Gamble for 3 years and was also a salesman for a small printing company for three years prior to starting Graphic Connections in 1992. But even during my time working for others, I was investing in real estate on the side. I've been using direct mail and direct response marketing for most of the 37 years I have been self-employed.

At Graphic Connections, we specialize in helping our clients design and implement effective direct mail campaigns. We also do the same thing for own marketing. I've experienced direct mail marketing from all three sides for most of my career. That is as a consumer, as a mailer for my own business, and helping my clients design and print their mailers.

Additionally, as I said in the introduction, I have been a real estate investor for 25 years as well. Although I don't flip houses on a daily basis, I have done it in the past, and I do hold rental property right now. That's a benefit to you, because we understand completely what it is you're looking for, and what you have to do to find and attract good leads. I am active in the real estate industry and involved with several different coaching and mastermind groups. This allows me to stay on top of the latest and most effective marketing systems and market trends.

We have a very hands-on approach at Graphic Connections Group, and I am always available if you have questions. You could not be in better hands.

Chapter 1

I Thought Direct Mail Was Dead!

*Direct Mail has never been dead.
It just took a backseat to digital marketing
for about 10 years. But it's back!*

How many times have you heard "Direct mail is dead!"?

Every time the post office raises rates, fewer people mail. Many people have the mistaken impression that increased postal rates make direct mail unaffordable.

We've been taught that online advertising and email marketing are the key to millions. "That old-fashioned mail stuff is for old folks." There are online gurus making a fortune everywhere. The allure of online marketing is exciting. Sending out a few emails and watching the money flow in is a concept that attracts many.

Some of that is true. However, if direct mail is dead, and online is the only way, why do we see almost every major online retailer spending millions of dollars on all types of media, <u>including</u> direct mail?

They're doing it because direct mail works. It works in just about every industry, but some better than others. **They're also doing it because they know a mixed approach is more effective than one single approach by itself.**

WHAT HAPPENED TO MAKE DIRECT MAIL APPEALING AGAIN?

I'm sure you can relate to getting hundreds, if not thousands of daily emails, most of which are unsolicited. Even the emails you agreed to receive are overwhelming. You have spam filters, but they don't catch it all. Half the time your spam filter catches a few emails that you want, so you end up having to search through the spam filter to find the good emails, which frustrates you more.

It seems like every time you buy something online, you end up with emails from at least 5 different companies. You start deleting as fast as you can. Often, legitimate offers that you might actually have an interest in get deleted.

There is no question that when email first got popular, and Google AdWords was still new, there was a window of opportunity during which you could focus strictly online and make a bucket of cash.

It is still possible, but it is getting more difficult every day. Plus, there are a lot of businesses that just don't work well online. Retail, restaurants, and service businesses have a tough time marketing strictly online.

To make matters worse, just when you think you have an online system figured out, the technology changes. Google often changes the rules, or a million other factors out of your control change, and it's back to the drawing board to come up with another strategy. In addition, email for business purposes is no longer free. Most auto-responder services charge fees that go up as you get more people on your list.

Pay-per-click advertising continues to get more expensive. It is not unusual to pay $10 per click or more for one key word. The cost of advertising online has skyrocketed, which makes earning a profit that much more difficult. It certainly has made it more complicated and risky.

Do you honestly look at every email in your inbox? Chances are you don't even look at one percent of them. You definitely don't look at those that come unsolicited.

To make it even more difficult, the legal system has stiff penalties for those who abuse email, and it is very easy to find yourself in an expensive legal battle when all you're trying to do is innocently promote your business.

LET'S TAKE A LOOK AT DIRECT MAIL IN CONTRAST TO ONLINE MARKETING.

FIRST, there are no laws against sending unsolicited, actual printed mail, to someone's physical mailbox. No one is damaged and it doesn't cost them a dime to receive mail. It is true that some people get irritated by junk mail. But it is not illegal, and you will not get in trouble sending it.

SECOND, even the busiest person eventually has to go to the mailbox, pick up the mail, and shuffle through it to decide what to keep and what to throw away. Okay, some of the busiest people don't look at their mail; they have someone else do it. But that doesn't mean you can't get their attention using mail. This is where you can use unique strategies, such as Lumpy Mail, to get through the gatekeeper and get the attention of your intended target.

You have at least a second or two to get their attention. It is very easy to delete an email without ever seeing a single word in the email. It is not so easy to get rid of a direct mail piece without at least taking a quick glance at it.

THIRD, most of us spend a good part of our day staring at the computer screen, and it gets tiring. There is still a large part of society that enjoys reading the printed word on paper. I rarely will read any sort of long document on the Internet, but I will take a long letter, or report, or a book, and read it in my easy chair.

LET ME GIVE YOU A FEW FACTS TO CHEW ON.

The Direct Marketing Association says that 73% of people prefer to receive a direct mail solicitation vs. an email solicitation.

50% of consumers say they pay more attention to postal mail than email (Epsilon Preference Study, 2011).

60% of consumers say they enjoy checking their mailbox and receiving mail (Epsilon Preference Study, 2011).

65% of consumers say they receive too many emails every day.

A fast-growing percentage of people express frustration and resentment with email marketing even from sources with which they have a good relationship (Alliance Research).

The preference for direct mail even extends to the 18 to 34 age group (Epsilon Preference Study, 2011).

98% of consumers retrieve their mail from the mailbox the day it is delivered and 77% sort through it the same day (USPS data, reported in DM news 2/11).

"Tangible materials such as direct mail trigger a much deeper level of emotional processing than any other media. They also generate more activity in the area of brain associated with integration of visual and facial information" ("Using Neuroscience to Understand the Role of Direct Mail", a study by Bangor University and Millward Brown). **This basically means direct mail has a better chance than any other media of motivating a person to take action.**

These Statistics Prove Direct Mail Is Not Dead. Not Only Is It Not Dead, But It Is Arguably More Effective At Creating An Emotional Connection With Potential Clients.

Many marketers are starting to use direct mail to drive people online. They are also doing the reverse—gathering leads using online methods, then using direct mail to close the deal. The sooner you can get people from your online system offline, the more effective your overall marketing system will be.

An ideal strategy is to use both direct mail and online marketing as a tag-team approach.

DIRECT MAIL IS ESPECIALLY EFFECTIVE IN REAL ESTATE.

Whether you are a real estate investor or agent, the same basic reasons apply. Most of you want to work specific geographical areas that you've chosen. It may be because it's close to your house. Perhaps because those areas are especially hot right now. It might be that those areas contain houses that typically have a lot of equity and are easy to flip. It could be the price range you are looking for. Whatever it is, the beauty of direct mail is you can find the physical address of your ideal prospect, and you can reach them directly by putting something in their mailbox. In comparison, finding the email addresses of potential homeowners who live in a specific area is extremely difficult. Even if you can find an email address, getting them to actually notice an email that you send is next to impossible.

Contrast that with direct mail, where you can develop a very targeted list, in a specific location, with specific demographics. There are other systems that will allow you to rent a list that can give you even more demographics, such as the value of the house, whether it has a mortgage, whether the mortgage is paid on time, the equity in the house, absentee owners, and a host of other factors. (Note: When you "rent" a list, you are paying a fee to the list owner for the rights to mail to that list a specified number of times.)

Both agents and investors can pick specific properties to target based on their own personal business criteria, and send them personalized direct mail pieces that speak directly to the owner, and in the terms they want them to hear.

The more narrow your list of ideal prospects, the better direct mail can be. The reason for this is if you really know who your target prospect is, and what they want, you can craft a specific direct mail message to speak to those needs. Contrast this with something like a radio advertisement, which is heard by anyone who is listening to that radio station. Yes it goes to a wide audience, but it is very difficult to deal with specific needs of a specific audience using that type of media.

Plus, if your target audience is a manageable number, you can afford to spend a lot for very extensive direct mail packages, with multiple touches. These can really be effective in getting the prospect's attention.

There's a reason why in just about every mailbox in America, people see postcards from real estate agents all the time. Those postcards will say Just Listed, Just Sold, Recent Sales in Your Area, etc. If you own a house that has high equity, or are behind on your mortgage, chances are you have received postcards or letters from other real estate investors offering to buy that house. These strategies have been used for decades,

and they continue to be used today more than any other marketing strategy in the real estate field. **The reason is, direct mail is alive and well, and it really works in real estate.**

Chapter 2

If You Are Not Using Direct Mail for Your REI Business, You Are Leaving Money on the Table.

This is an area where many REI's make a huge mistake. They get hung up on the attractiveness and sometimes low cost of digital marketing. It may be social media, email, fancy websites, lead generation programs, pay-per-click, Google retargeting, or whatever. Don't get me wrong, I am not saying that these types of marketing are not effective. I am not criticizing them in any way. In fact, I think a comprehensive marketing program should have multiple different ways to contact a prospect.

However, one point that people miss can result in you missing out on a very large segment of the market. There is a reason direct mail has worked for years and continues to work for the real estate investment industry. It has to do with the demographics of your ideal prospect. For most REI's, an ideal prospect has high equity, has lived in their house for a long time, and the house is run down. What demographic fits those criteria a high percentage of the time? Answer: Older people. Take it one step further—many deals come from houses that are vacated due to people moving into retirement homes, or downsizing, or the owner has died, and an heir has a house that they don't know what to do with.

It is a fact that most older people are not necessarily the most digitally savvy. Yes, today most people do have a cell phone. But the older generation does not tend to be addicted to their cell phone like the rest of us. They tend not to be computer savvy. But they do value the written word on paper. They do read their mail. Many of them read every word of every piece of mail. They value personalization and handwritten correspondence.

The fact is if you don't use direct mail as one of your marketing strategies, there's a good chance that you will never reach that segment of the market. You may do well with your digital marketing, but you're still limiting yourself to the people who tend to respond to digital advertising. The other benefit of direct mail, which I've already discussed, is that you can buy a list that targets the exact demographic that I mentioned. You're going to be mailing to people that tend to look favorably upon direct mail.

The headline is correct. If you are not using direct mail as part of your marketing mix you are leaving money on the table. Big money! Don't make that mistake!

I THOUGHT EMAIL AND WEB ADVERTISING WERE CHEAPER.

Since anyone can send a single email basically free of charge, the perception is that email marketing is much cheaper than direct mail marketing. On the surface, that is true. But let's dig a little deeper.

First of all, as I said earlier, sending single emails through your own email account is free in most cases. However, most marketing systems utilize an auto-responder, and those systems are not free. The more emails you send, the more it costs. Often, you'll need more than one auto-responder system to manage various campaigns. Different systems have different pros and cons, and the more sophisticated you get in your marketing, the more difficult it becomes to find one that can do it all for you.

Second, renting a targeted email list is far more expensive than renting a targeted physical mailing list. Even if you can find an email list to rent, which is hit and miss at best, the email addresses change constantly, and deliverability is extremely low. The only way to email a cold list is to find a paid service willing to take the legal risk. These services are often very expensive. Plus, the recipients are not very receptive for all the aforementioned reasons.

If you don't buy an email list, you have to get a lead some other way online. Yes, organic search is possible. If you don't know what organic search means, I am talking about going to Google or Yahoo and searching for a given topic. Organics are the results that come up, usually around the middle of the page, just below the paid ads. Organic search is free, but getting noticed is not easy. You have to be on the first page of Google to have a chance.

There are thousands of companies that will take your money and promise to help you get noticed. They call that SEO, which stands for Search Engine Optimization. It is extremely expensive and time-consuming to get any kind of results with SEO. And it does not

happen overnight. It takes months, often years, to get ranked on the first page of Google for important keywords. (There is no guarantee you will ever get to the first page.)

And yes, in the real estate field there are all sorts of online systems that promise to generate leads. Many of them are effective. But for all the reasons I mentioned earlier, they are not targeted. That means if you want to work in a specific area and target specific addresses, it is almost impossible to do that online. With online systems, you have to wait for people to come to you. You are depending totally on the chance that someone happens to find your webpage, and they happen to live in the area you are targeting, and they happen to be interested enough to opt-in to your webpage.

Once they opt-in to your webpage, you have permission to market to them via email or other means. But the chance of all that happening without you spending significant money on online advertising is slim.

WITH DIRECT MAIL, YOU CAN REACH OUT TO THEM.

There are many choices for online advertising, in all different price ranges. The most popular is pay-per-click advertising, commonly done through Google. Paying for clicks can be very expensive. These days most common search terms in just about any industry go for more than $10 per click. It doesn't take very long to spend thousands, even tens of thousands of dollars, just getting people to go to your website. And there's no guarantee that they will read anything, or opt-in to your mailing list after they click. Opt-in rates can vary, depending on what you're asking the person to do. But anything over 10% is considered insanely high.

> **The bottom line is even though online marketing seems inexpensive on the surface, by the time you add up all these various costs, it can be <u>extremely</u> expensive.**

Online marketing is effective after a lead has requested more information from you. At that time you're free to send all the emails you want using fairly cost-effective systems. But again, it is not free.

Direct mail is a cost-effective way to get people's attention. **Using direct mail to generate interested prospects, then following up with online tools can be an extremely powerful marketing system.**

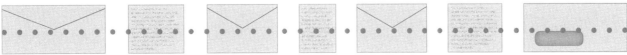

LET'S RUN THROUGH SOME NUMBERS.

A typical direct mail campaign might cost you, in rough numbers, one dollar per mail piece. Let's say you mail 1,000 mail pieces and spend $1,000. Let's say you got a 2% response rate, which is 20 people responding to your offer to buy their house.

Essentially it cost you $50 per lead. Let's also say you have an effective sales team that can close 10% of the leads. Let's say a typical sale for you could deliver a profit of at least $10,000. In this example you would close 2 leads, and profit $20,000. So you spent $1,000 and earned $20,000 in return. I would say that is a good return.

Now let's look at a typical online scenario. Let's say you decide to do a pay-per-click campaign, and wanted to get 20 leads to opt-into your website. Let's also assume the typical price per click is $10. It is not unusual for an online campaign to require 20 clicks for every 1 opt-in. Using that scenario, to get 20 leads online, it would require 400 clicks, at $10 per click, or $4,000 to get the same 20 leads you got with the direct mail piece.

If you assume you're a much better marketer and can get one opt-in for every 10 clicks, which is a 10% opt-in rate, it would still take you 200 clicks to get 20 leads. At $10 per click, that is $2,000. This is double the cost of the direct mail campaign.

Plus, and this is a big deal, online marketing is not targeted. That means even though you may get a lot of leads, you'll have a much lower closing rate because a lot of the leads will be completely outside the market you are looking for. You would be lucky to do half as well with online leads as you do with targeted direct mail leads.

Of course there are other options for online advertising, and they all have different rates. But few can be as effective as direct mail, when you really break down the true cost of the entire campaign.

CONSUMERS PREFER "SNAIL" MAIL OVER EMAIL.

For you younger folks who never heard of "snail mail," let me explain. When email first came out, traditional postal mail was given the nickname "snail mail," mainly because it was not instantaneous like email.

Let's get back to why consumers prefer "snail mail."

There are several reasons for this. First, it is simply easier to read something printed on paper than on the computer screen. This is especially true for the real estate investor

market. A lot of the houses that you will buy and sell, will be from people who are older and have their house paid off. It's a fact that older people definitely prefer more old-fashioned methods over modern methods. Paper and ink almost always rules with older people. The more personalized, even handwritten, is better in most cases.

Second, you can do things with paper and ink, such as adding scents, special papers, incredibly rich photos, Lumpy Mail and other things that create an emotional response, that you can't do on a computer screen.

Another benefit is that people can put direct mail aside and come back to it and read it later. I often collect my mail and save it for my next airline flight. I will go through it in more detail on the plane. Technically you can do the same thing with an email, but that is much more difficult to do given the information overload that we all face. Plus, if you get an email on your desktop at the office, unless you have a very sophisticated mobile device and understand cloud systems, it is difficult to take an email received in one place and read it later on another device.

I spend all day in front of the computer screen. I actually enjoy getting away from it, and reading things on good old-fashioned paper. It's relaxing to sit in my easy chair and read mail, magazines, catalogs, etc. I am not the only one who feels this way.

Lastly, a direct mail piece can be shared with other people much more easily than an email. Not that you can't send an email easily, but for all the reasons mentioned before, we all face information overload in our inbox. If you want someone's opinion on a direct mail piece, handing it to them and asking them to read it has a much better chance of getting their attention.

Chapter 3

What Business Are You In?

You are in the marketing business,
whether you like it or not!

Now that we've established that direct mail still is an effective marketing tool in today's market, let's step back for a minute and talk about basic marketing.

Before you can embark on any type of marketing campaign, especially a direct mail marketing campaign, you need to understand all the variables that will affect your success. That all starts with understanding your business and what you're really selling.

The single most important thing you need to understand is...

You are in the marketing business,
whether you like it or not!

LET ME EXPLAIN.

You may identify yourself as a real estate investor, but you are really in the marketing business. No matter how good you are at your trade, if you don't have any customers, you don't have a business. Learning how to attract and acquire customers is necessary in every business, and is the single most important criterion to success in every business.

Your product or service is important, and a vital element, but it is secondary. You can hire people to do what you do fairly easily. Don't get your feelings hurt. It doesn't mean you're not important, and not good at what you do. The point is fulfilling the actual work that needs to be done to deliver a product or service is usually the easy part. Doctors who have more patients than they can handle can hire more doctors. Law firms who have too many cases can hire more lawyers. Retailers can hire more clerks. Real estate firms can hire more agents. Manufacturers can make more products. All that is the easy part. (Unless you possess some skill that no one else has, and in that case you probably don't have a marketing problem. But that is not the norm.)

In almost every industry, finding someone to do the work is the easy part. But hiring a person to get you more customers is not so easy. It is far easier to find someone with a specific skill than it is to find a person who can market and sell. And even if you are good at finding someone who can sell, typically having a marketing system in place is critical to the success of the salesperson. The particular skill of developing marketing systems is extremely hard to find.

You might think all you have to do is hire some good salespeople and that will solve your problem. Ask any business owner who has tried to hire salespeople and he or she will tell you differently. The only way to be successful in hiring salespeople is to first have a marketing system in place that drives leads to the sales force. It is critical that the system works in such a way that clients or patients are attracted to you. You want them knocking on your door, wanting your product or service. That way you do not need superstar salespeople to close the deal. If your business relies on having superstar salespeople to both find and close leads, you are going to struggle to succeed.

The best person to become the marketing expert is you, the business owner—especially when the business is small. Even medium and large businesses require the people at the top to be savvy marketers. The sooner you can accept the fact that the most important thing you can do is to learn how to be an effective marketer, the sooner you'll be on the road to success greater than you've ever achieved before.

YOU MARKET OR YOU DIE.

That may sound a bit harsh, but it is the truth of any business. Every successful business needs a steady stream of new prospects and customers coming to the door every week and month. No matter how good you are, you will lose business over time. You have to constantly be replacing those customers you lose, and if you want to grow you have to get new customers on top of that.

The days of sitting back and hoping for people to come to you are over. In this market, people have too many options, including going online for just about every product or service imaginable. In the real estate field it's the same. Not only are all sorts of online services available for every aspect of real estate transaction, there are thousands of new and excited real estate investors popping up every single weekend all across America. Those people are coming from weekend seminars put on by real estate gurus teaching them how to get rich flipping houses.

Granted, 95% of those people will not get off first base in the business, but there are so many flooding the market, **the only way you can succeed is to have strategic and consistent marketing.**

Let me tell you, if you are one of those people who just came from a real estate seminar, and you're super excited, I congratulate you. I'll tell you the same thing that the "guru" likely told you. If you don't get serious right now, and commit a substantial amount of time and resources to regular marketing, month after month after month, you will not succeed. This is not a "work 2 hours and get rich" business.

But the good news is, those who are serious, and those who use the strategies that I'll be presenting to you shortly, not only succeed, they succeed in big ways. Their lives are changed beyond their wildest imaginations.

To be successful in business in today's market, you must invest a percentage of your cash, each month, in a consistent and predictable marketing program. You must find ways to attract new customers to come to you over your competition. You need to put a system in place where the prospects are calling you. Then you can have your salesforce (or you) talk to them and close sales. If you don't, your business will die. It's that simple.

You also have to be more creative than ever before. You need to use as many different media sources as possible to generate prospects. Because different people respond to different things, using a diverse mix of media is smart business.

But here's the really good news. You don't have to think of this yourself. You have guys like me, and other real estate and direct mail experts that I work with, out there thinking of, and testing, new ideas all the time. You just have to implement the ideas that seem to fit you best.

WHAT DOES A TYPICAL MARKETING PLAN LOOK LIKE?

You need to have two different marketing funnels. What is a marketing funnel?
A marketing funnel is a series of steps that systematically draws a prospect or customer through the buying process.

You need to have a funnel for prospects, and you need to have a funnel for existing customers. You need two because you handle these two different groups of people in different ways.

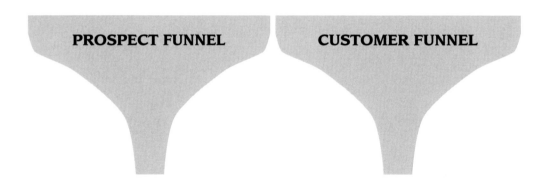

Now before we get into these two types of funnels, you will be asking yourself, "How can I have existing customers if I'm flipping houses?" That's a valid question. The answer is, it depends on how you plan to do business. If you're someone who just wants to buy a house at wholesale, fix it up, and then flip it retail, you probably won't have existing customers. Sure, as you begin to sell houses, you will develop a list of clients who bought from you. And over time, that list could be valuable if you're looking to sell the same person multiple houses. But that is a long-term play. So in your case, you may only need one funnel for now. That will be the prospect funnel.

But let's say you are planning to buy houses at wholesale, and then flip them to other real estate investors who are going to fix them up and either hold them or sell them at retail. In that case, chances are you will find customers that will come back and buy from you again and again. So in that case, you may have two funnels, a prospect funnel, and an existing customer funnel. Let's go ahead and talk about both.

With prospects, you need to introduce them to your product or service, and entice them to try you out. With existing customers, you need to stay in front of them so they don't forget you, and also to encourage them to spend more than they are already spending. Your best source of additional revenue is always your existing customers. Too many businesses ignore existing customers and spend all their marketing dollars on finding new clients.

It's ten times easier to get more from an existing customer, or reactivate a past customer who has stopped buying from you, than it is to get a new prospect to buy from you. But both funnels are very important.

WHAT ARE MY MARKETING CHOICES FOR REAL ESTATE?

Of course, direct mail is not the only method of marketing for real estate investors. Earlier we discussed some online choices. You can also use roadside signs often called "bandit signs." You can use door hangers. You can make cold calls. You can knock on doors and talk to people. You can put ads in the newspaper. You can do billboards. You can put up posters on free bulletin boards around town. The sky is the limit if you use your imagination.

However, we also know that each one of those methods has pluses and minuses. I'll just give you a few words on each of these methods.

Online Marketing ·

Can be very expensive, especially with pay-per-click advertising. This is not targeted. You will have very little control over the flow of leads.

Bandit Signs ·

Fairly inexpensive, but are banned in many communities. You can face stiff fines if you're caught using them in communities where they are banned. They don't stay up very long, so you have to replace them constantly. They're also not targeted, so you'll get a lot of calls from people that don't fit your criteria.

Door Hangers

Door hangers are similar to direct mail in that you can target specific houses. They're also good because people will look at something hanging on their doorknob. But distributing door hangers can be expensive and time-consuming. It's typically less expensive to mail something to a house than to pay someone to hang a door hanger.

Cold Calling and Door Knocking

Cold calling is extremely difficult in today's society. Between the do-not-call list, and caller ID, it's almost impossible to get through to someone who doesn't know you. Door knocking doesn't have the same restrictions, but there are very few people who have the guts to go door-to-door, plus it is very slow. It takes a special kind of person who is willing to do either of these methods. But if you're that kind of person, they can be effective.

Billboards

Billboards can be very expensive, but will generate a lot of leads. They're not targeted so you spent a whole lot of time weeding through people who waste your time. This is typically not a good strategy for beginners.

Direct Mail

For all the reasons I mentioned already, direct mail is probably the easiest and most manageable marketing system that checks off the most boxes. It is targeted. It's affordable. It's duplicatable. You can set up a system that will run for months and forget about it. And it's scalable. Almost every successful real estate investor uses direct mail as part of their marketing system.

LET'S LOOK AT A TYPICAL DIRECT MAIL MARKETING FUNNEL FOR BOTH PROSPECTS AND CUSTOMERS.

The Prospect Funnel

Send out postcards or sales letters to a specific target market that you have developed from Kent's SMART SUITE software. In most cases, you'll be offering to buy their house for cash, close fast and make the deal super easy for the client. You either have a phone number for them to call, an email address, a website, or all three. The format of the mailer is typically a postcard, a handwritten letter, or a business letter. If you're really aggressive, you can use Lumpy Mail, which is extremely effective for super targeted lists. (Lumpy Mail

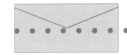

is sending something unusual, that has a "lump" or a dimension to it, in the mail.) The method you use depends on the type of clients you are going after. We see success from all four types of mailers.

When they call, in most cases you interview them on the phone with a series of planned questions. The objective is to set up an appointment with the prospect who fits your criteria. You may be more sophisticated, and send them to a landing page where they can opt-in for some sort of free report, or more information. After they opt-in you can start sending them a series of emails that will continually remind them to call you if they're interested in selling their house. Since you mailed to them in the first place, you can look up their name in your database, and then mail them follow-up letters that are even more personalized or specific based on how you sell.

It is extremely important to hit cold prospects more than once. There are all sorts of studies that show that frequency improves response. Studies also show that it takes anywhere from 3 to 13 touches for a prospect to respond. I realize that's a wide range. It is wide because the studies come from all different industries, with all different offers, and it is impossible to nail down a statistic like that exactly. But the statistics don't lie. Those who mail to the same lead more than once do better than those who mail only once.

In our experience, the clients who are most successful mail to the same list between three and seven times. Some believe in hitting the client every week with increasingly harder hitting messages. Others believe that stretching out the contact over a period of months is better. I have seen campaigns succeed using both strategies.

The Customer Funnel

For customers, many of the same rules apply, except since they've already bought from you, your offers will likely be different. And your frequency will be more spread out. Since the customer already knows you, you don't need to hit them every week. But you do have to hit them often enough that they don't forget about you—I would say a minimum of two times per year with some sort of correspondence. Here's where you can use email effectively. You can also use newsletters, direct mail postcards, and sales letters. Lumpy Mail is also an excellent customer funnel tool.

Your goal should be to upsell them on additional product purchases from you. Your objective is to extend the lifetime value of each customer. A secondary goal is to make sure that they do not forget about you the next time they are ready to purchase something you sell.

POSTAGE

Should you mail First-class mail or Marketing (formerly called standard or bulk) mail?

First of all, let me clarify the confusion in terminology. The post office is constantly changing their terms. Years ago, the cheapest possible way to mail was called bulk mail. About 10 years ago, they decided to change the name to standard mail. Recently, they changed it again to marketing mail. All three of those terms mean the same thing - cheaper mail. If you are confused, don't feel bad. Everyone is.

The main difference between first-class and marketing (standard or bulk) mail is price and speed of delivery. In general, first-class costs around $.20 more per piece than marketing mail for most letter or large postcard mailings. The post office gives you a discount in exchange for allowing them to take more time to deliver the piece. They also do not return the bad addresses in marketing mail. Marketing mail can take anywhere from 1 to 4 weeks to be delivered, depending on how far away the delivery point is from the mail drop. (Note that in most cases, it usually takes 7-14 days.)

If time is of the essence, use first-class. You don't have enough control over delivery times using marketing mail.

In general, first-class mail, using live stamps, will pull better than marketing mail. Stamps, first-class or marketing, will pull better than preprinted indicia. This has been the conventional wisdom for many years.

However, there are exceptions. If you're sending postcards, or other obvious mail pieces that are clearly marketing materials, it is not really necessary to use first-class stamps. No one is going to confuse a marketing postcard with a personal letter, so you might as well save the postage and send it out standard mail with an indicia. That is, of course, if you are in no hurry. If your offer is time critical, you may want to spend the money for first-class anyway just to ensure it gets there on time.

If you're sending a letter, stamps are almost always the preferred method for the best response rates. However, many direct-mail companies, including ours, have ways to use standard mail stamps along with a cancellation that looks like a first-class cancellation that gives the impression of first-class stamps. We have tested this side-by-side with first-class stamps and have not seen any difference in response. But again, standard mail takes longer, so you if you are in a hurry, first-class is always the best way to go.

In general, when we design a mail piece, we look at the strategy we are using, and the prospect we are targeting, and then choose the best postage method that we feel will achieve the most cost effective results.

 First Class Stamp for Letters
1-7 days from drop date

 First Class Presort Stamp for Postcards
1-7 days from drop date

 First Class Stamp for Postcards
1-7 days from drop date

 First Class Presort Indicia
1-7 days from drop date

 Marketing - Standard - Bulk Mail Stamp
7-14 days from drop date

 Marketing - Standard - Bulk Mail Indicia
7-14 days from drop date

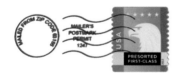 **First Class Presort Stamp with Fake First Class Cancel (Looks like full First Class)**
1-7 days from drop date

 **Marketing - Standard - Bulk Mail Stamp with Fake First Class Cancel (Looks like First Class)**
7-14 days from drop date

Chapter 4

Key Elements to Success in Marketing

"Response is one of the five maxims of successful direct marketing. And if you have that, the other four don't matter."

I'm assuming you now understand the importance of being an expert marketer. Before you can decide if online or direct mail marketing makes sense for you, you need to understand the basic elements of any marketing campaign.

There are twelve key elements to every successful direct marketing campaign. These elements are true both for offline and online marketing. Unfortunately, most people miss out on some, if not all, of these key characteristics.

KEY ELEMENT #1: HAVE A UNIQUE SELLING PROPOSITION (USP)

Dan Kennedy is one of the greatest marketing geniuses of the last 30 years. I will quote him when it comes to defining a USP. Dan says, "What is it that you do that would make the customer choose you over anyone else, including doing nothing? And you can't use price, quality, or service."

You have to ZIG when everyone else ZAGS. What is your ZIG?

Everybody claims to offer the lowest prices, the best quality, and the best service. Consumers have come to expect that from everyone. It is not unique. What is it that you do that sets you apart from your competition?

Dan uses the example of Domino's pizza. Domino's never talked about how good their pizza was, the quality of their ingredients, or anything else about the pizza. All they said was, "Hot pizza delivered in 30 minutes or less, guaranteed." Good pizza was not part of the equation. They built an empire on the promise to deliver it within 30 minutes. The customers cared more about the speed than they did about anything else.

Finding your unique selling proposition is perhaps the most difficult thing for any business to do. As a real estate investor, you buy houses for cash, just like everyone else. Almost all of your competitors offer the same thing. Does this sound familiar?

We will buy your house for cash.　　　**No repairs.**

No real estate commissions.　　　**We will close fast.**

Everyone is saying the same thing. What can you do that makes you stand out from the hundreds of other people all saying the same thing?

A more compelling USP is "We Buy Ugly Houses." It uniquely differentiates the offer from all the others in the industry.

Another great example of a USP in a name is 1-800-SELL-NOW. It is both a phone number and also a name that is easy to remember.

Maybe you come up with a unique guarantee. Maybe you give your service a name that stands out. Maybe you have a slightly different approach than your competitors. Think about what you do and how you do it and find a way to differentiate yourself.

24

One example in the real estate space is the headline, "I will sell your house in 90 days or less or I'll buy it myself." That truly is a unique, compelling message for anyone interested in selling their house.

Once you've decided how you are unique, you need to build your marketing message around that USP.

Note that having a unique design can help to separate you from competitors if your unique selling proposition is similar. For instance, having a photo of a house on the mailer and allowing a text response is unique and will set you apart.

CHECKLIST FOR IDENTIFYING USP

Below is a list of topics that will help you to identify what is unique about your product or service. Remember saying that you have the best price, quality, or service does not count.

- ☐ Unique Name
- ☐ competitive positioning
- ☐ exclusive niche
- ☐ affinity
- ☐ hidden benefit
- ☐ method of marketing and distribution
- ☐ continuity
- ☐ membership
- ☐ added value
- ☐ premiums/gift with purchase
- ☐ packaging difference
- ☐ size
- ☐ expertise
- ☐ payment terms
- ☐ guarantee
- ☐ celebrity
- ☐ combination

That doesn't mean that using the same offers as your competition won't work.

Don't get me wrong. Everything I said above is absolutely true, and if you can uniquely package your message, you will absolutely stand out above your competition, and your results will be better than theirs. But we mail out postcards and letters every single day that say the same thing. They all have some version of "I will buy your house for cash, close fast, and make it easy for you." In those cases, those clients still succeed if they mail regularly to good targeted lists and mail frequently. You see, you can also out-market your competition by staying in front of your potential prospects more than they do, even if your message is similar.

But we have clients who have taken the advice above, differentiate themselves, and their results are stellar. The "1-800-SELL-NOW" clients do extremely well with that slogan.

KEY ELEMENT #2: IDENTIFY YOUR TARGET MARKET OR CLIENT.

Perhaps the greatest thing about direct mail marketing is that it is very easy to target specific demographic groups. You can rent lists that contain just about any criteria you can imagine about a market. On the consumer side, it is common to look for specific ZIP Codes, income levels, the value of homes, equity in the home, type of family, size of family, owners or renters, and a myriad of other demographic factors.

On the commercial side, you would look for locations, square footage, SIC codes, size of business, number of employees, location, annual sales, etc.

WHO SHOULD YOU TARGET?

Choosing the right list is vital to the success of a direct marketing campaign. You can mail the greatest offer in the world to the wrong list and get zero response. You can also mail a mediocre offer to a good list and still get a good response.

There are three main types of targets that every business should approach:

Your in-house customer list   **Your targeted cold prospect list**

Your in-house prospect list

The in-house customer list is obvious. It is simply a list of your customers. So many marketers take this list for granted and don't do anything with their customers. Never forget your in-house customer list, as it is just as important as any other list you may use.

The in-house prospect list contains prospects who have contacted you in the past about your product or service, but have not bought from you. The fact that they already took a step to contact you puts you closer to a sale. Just because they haven't bought yet doesn't mean they don't like you. They may still be thinking about it. Maybe you didn't do a good enough job of showing them the value proposition, and can do a better job the second time around. Maybe they never really saw your materials even though they inquired. Maybe you just did a lousy job the first time around. No matter what the reason, this is a very valuable list.

The third list is a targeted cold prospect list. This one is a little more difficult to obtain, and you have to put on your thinking cap to figure out who exactly should be on this list. In order to do this, you have to identify your ideal target customer, and the demographics associated with them. Then go to sources where you can find people who meet those criteria. There are mailing list companies, magazines, associations, clubs, trade groups, and all sorts of sources for people with similar demographics.

A good example of this in the real estate business would be choosing high equity properties. Let's say you do not target your list properly, and most of the people you mail to have very little equity in their property. To make money as a real estate investor, you have to purchase houses at wholesale value, often 50 cents on the dollar or less. If you offer a person who owes $100,000 on their house $50,000, there is almost no chance they're going to say yes. You may even get a 10% response rate to the mailer, because you have a compelling offer. But if none of those people are the right prospects, you will not get any deals. You are wasting your money even soliciting those types of people.

But it's not enough just to target the right prospects...

KEY ELEMENT #3: HAVE AN IRRESISTIBLE OFFER

An irresistible offer is the lifeblood of any marketing campaign. So many people make a mistake of sending out a mail piece, email, ad, or website that has no offer at all. Typically people will say, "We are in the _____ business and here's our phone number." That is not an offer.

It is critical to determine what your objective is, and then craft an offer to help you achieve that objective. If your goal is to generate a lead, an example of an irresistible offer might be, "Call today for your free report on how to maximize profits when selling your house." An even stronger offer might be, "Call me today for a no obligation cash offer on your house." or "Text this code to get an instant cash offer." Another super powerful offer is to send an actual check (fake check) with an offer to a homeowner.

So many people make the mistake of only listing features and benefits, but they are missing a compelling offer. To say "We buy houses" and list a phone number is not an offer.

KEY ELEMENT #4: ALWAYS TALK IN TERMS OF BENEFITS TO THE PROSPECT TO SOLVE THEIR KEY PROBLEM

Any time you write anything on any sort of marketing piece, ask the question, "Who cares?" When I say who cares, I mean look at it from the prospect's point of view. If the prospect doesn't care about what you just said, don't say it.

Let's look at the real estate business again. What is a typical problem someone might have? They may have a vacant house that is costing them money, and they don't know what to do. Think about that problem when you craft your message. You might say, "We will remove all the worry and hassle of fixing up and getting your vacant house ready for sale, so you can move on and enjoy your family." A statement like that is solving their key problem by talking about the benefit to them.

KEY ELEMENT #5: CREATE A SENSE OF URGENCY

Sense of urgency is very important in any marketing piece, but especially a direct mail piece. Create a sense of urgency by creating a specific time or a specific deadline. You can create scarcity with, "This offer is limited to the first 10 people! Respond within 48 hours!" or "We are only buying one house in your neighborhood." Sense of urgency motivates the reader to act. It is human nature to not want to miss out. The more you can make it feel like the reader will be missing out, the stronger your message will be.

KEY ELEMENT #6: INCLUDE A CALL TO ACTION

A call to action tells them exactly what to do and when to do it. "Pick up the phone and call our office today" is a very simple call to action. You might say, "Go to our website and fill out the form today." Working in the call to action with the sense of urgency is a powerful duo.

Note that having a texting option in your call to action is a great way to increase response rates. Plus it is unique, which will help set you apart.

KEY ELEMENT #7: INCLUDE A GUARANTEE

If you can't guarantee what you sell, you'd better find a different business.

Having a guarantee takes the risk away from the prospect. Most people do not like to take any risk, especially when it comes to receiving a solicitation in the mail. This is also true of online solicitations. We all have an inherent distrust of people trying to get our money, so guarantees go a long way to help relieve that distrust. The stronger your guarantee can be, the stronger response rates will be. The strongest guarantee is always a 100% money back guarantee. However, that is not always possible in every sale situation. For instance, if someone was unhappy with a real estate transaction, there is no way you could guarantee their money back.

What you can do is guarantee various elements of the transaction. Here are some ideas.

I guarantee I will call you back in 24 hours with a cash offer.

I guarantee I'll fix anything that goes wrong for the first year.

I guarantee I'll show up with cash-money on your doorstep at the time I make the offer.

I guarantee I'll call you back with a smile on my face.

I guarantee you will have no hassles and the transaction will close quickly.

There are all kinds of things you can do with guarantees to strengthen your offer.

KEY ELEMENT #8: HAVE A FOLLOW-UP SYSTEM IN PLACE

All the previous elements dealt with the mail piece itself. However, it is just as critical to have an effective follow-up system in place. Getting a bunch of responses to a mail piece is a complete waste of money if you don't follow up properly. This means when you first get a response, you need to have a way to do something that really gets the attention of the prospect. You might send them a "shock-and-awe" kit. A shock-and-awe kit is a box of goodies the prospect would never expect to get from anyone in the situation. You might

make a personal appearance. A phone call from the president. Anything you can do to tell the prospect you care is a good thing.

Beyond the initial contact, you also need to have an ongoing follow-up system in place. An email auto-responder would be effective in this case. But you can also do it with additional direct mail pieces. Maybe a quarterly newsletter. Maybe periodic phone calls. Whatever works for your market to ensure that people remember you is good.

In real estate, you can exponentially increase your profits by spending a fair amount of money and time focusing on maximizing closing ratios. Even a small increase in back-end closing rates can return you tens, if not hundreds of thousands of incremental profit dollars.

Do Not Skimp On This Step!

KEY ELEMENT #9: REPETITION IS EVERYTHING

Another key element is repetition. Repetition is King. If you think you can do one mail piece or one email campaign and set profit records, you're dreaming. In the case of real estate it's a fact that about 7% of the population moves every year. There's probably another 7% thinking about moving at any given time. That's only about 14% of the people who probably have any interest at all in hearing about selling their house. 14% means 14 out of 100, which means 86 out of 100 are probably not interested at all right now – even if you pull a good targeted list.

Next year another 7% of people are going to move and probably another 7% will be thinking about moving, so just because they're not interested this year does not mean they won't be interested next year.

> **Your goal as a marketer is to put your name in front of people often enough so that when it finally comes time for them to act, they think of you first before they think of your competition.**

Here's a rule of thumb. Whatever response you get from one mailer, you can at least double the response by doing two additional mail pieces. In other words, if you send the same thing three times to the same list, you'll typically get double the response you would get over just one mailing.

Another rule of thumb in direct mail is if an offer works, mail it again and again until it stops working. It is not uncommon to mail the same offer, to the same list, up to 10 times, before it finally gets to the point where it's no longer profitable to mail.

This is especially true in the real estate investing market these days. There are hundreds, if not thousands, of gurus traveling the country putting on weekend seminars teaching people how to flip houses. Almost every one of these guys teaches people to mail small postcards and simple handwritten letters to find houses to buy. They're also teaching people to look for high equity homes in certain areas, and all the students are being taught the same thing. They're even being pushed to the same web services who offer the same postcards to all different types of people.

Most of these people will not succeed. Not because the system doesn't work, but because they won't do the work to follow the system. They will do one mail piece, and never repeat. By hitting the prospect several times, ideally with mail pieces a little different than your competition (using the lessons taught above), you'll begin to build a brand with the recipient and they may begin to remember you. If you use the eight previous elements, you will stand out from most of your competition, because very few of them are doing these things. A typical mail sequence might look like:

Mailer #1: Small gcPowerMail Postcard	Mailer #2: Small Handwritten Postcard	Mailer #3: Handwritten Yellow Letter	Mailer #4: Business Letter

Mailer #5: Handwritten
Invitation Style Note

Mailer #6: Oversized
"Final Notice" Postcard

So remember: Mail, mail, mail, and then mail some more!

KEY ELEMENT #10: TRACK YOUR RESULTS

Failure to track results is perhaps the biggest mistake most marketers make. They will spend thousands of dollars on campaigns, but fail to put the systems in place to know who responded to those campaigns. Without proper tracking mechanisms, there is no way to know what worked and what didn't work. Successful marketers are constantly testing and tweaking their campaigns to continually improve.

There are various ways to track campaigns. If your offer asks for a phone call to respond, the simplest way is to have the person answering the phone ask them where they heard about your product or service. The problem with this method is people often forget to do that or they don't write it down, and before you know it you don't have the proper information.

Another way to do that is to get a tracking phone number. There are systems that allow you to buy phone numbers and use a specific phone number for a specific mail piece so you know the call that came in on that line could've only been from that mail piece. This is a good system but doing this for every mail piece individually can be challenging. It is a little easier to break up your mailings into groups or campaigns, then assign an individual phone number to a campaign.

Another method is to send people to a website that is a specific landing page for your specific offer. This is an excellent way to track, but does involve creating different landing

pages for each mail piece. Again, if you don't have an easy system to do this, it can be challenging. What often happens is people get in a hurry and they skip this step.

Perhaps the easiest method is to have a specific response device in the mail piece that gets mailed or faxed back to you. Some people consider this to be old-fashioned marketing, but it is very effective for tracking and some people still prefer to do business this way.

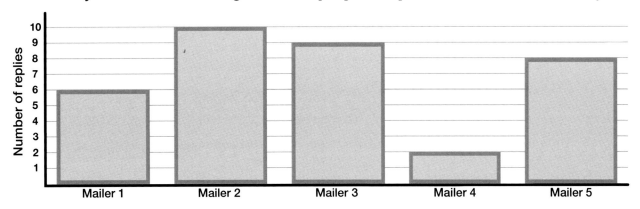

KEY ELEMENT #11: PERSONALIZE

It is a fact that personalization increases response rates no matter what your marketing method. The more you can talk specifically to the prospect, using their name or things about them, the better chance you have of connecting and getting them to respond. With today's technology, this step is easy.

Use "Dear Bob" instead of "Dear Friend."

Use "I want to buy your house at 123 Main St." instead of "I want to buy your house."

Include a picture of their actual house instead of a generic picture.

You get the idea. Any mailer worth his salt can personalize anything you want to whatever degree you want. It does typically add a little bit of cost, but it is well worth it.

KEY ELEMENT #12: UNDERSTAND THE NUMBERS OF MARKETING

All of the previous elements are important, but this one is perhaps the most important of all. Moreover, it is incredible to me how many people just don't get it. They don't think about the basic math of marketing.

They start a business, but never stop to think about what it's actually going to take to be successful in that business. In real estate, everybody gets hung up on how much money house flippers make. They watch the shows on TV where a good looking couple earns $85,000 on one flip and they have a ton of fun doing it. What they never think about is what it takes to get to the point where you even have a deal.

You see, to close enough deals to have a viable business, you have to generate enough prospects to give yourself a chance to close the deals. Let me give you a few numbers to think about.

Based on what we see in our business, all across the nation, most real estate investors require somewhere between 15 and 30 leads to close one deal. The most common number I hear is one in 25.

That means if you want to close one deal, chances are you're going to need to talk to 25 people who have raised their hands with interest in possibly allowing you to buy their house.

The next question is what's it going to take to get 25 leads? If you're using direct mail, it's a simple mathematical equation, and it all starts with what you think your response rate is going to be. I can tell you that based on what we see from doing thousands of mailings nationwide, most people generate between a .5% and 1.5% response rate. Yes, there is an occasional spike to 4%, and there's also a rare 0%. The majority of people settle somewhere in the neighborhood of 1% when they average their results over time. So let's use 1% as our number for this example.

If you need 25 leads, and you get a 1% response rate from your mailings, it's going to take you 2,500 pieces of mail to get 25 leads. That math is 2,500 × .01 = 25.

Yet we see people all the time mailing 100 postcards. I would say that 80% of the orders we get are for fewer than 500 mailers.

Let's do some more math. 1% of 100 equals one. 1% of 500 equals five. If it takes somewhere between 15 and 25 leads to get one deal, what are the chances you're going to get a deal if you only get one lead? What are the possibilities if you only get five leads?

Of course, you could get lucky, and that one lead could be a home run, and you could get a deal. I have had more than one person get two deals from fewer than 500 mailers. However, that is the rare exception and is not too far from the odds of winning the lottery.

This is the reason 80 to 90% of wannabe real estate investors generally drop out after their first mailing—because they don't generate enough leads to get a deal, and they give up before they even get started.

So before you even think about doing your first mailing, take a look at some basic math. Establish a plan that makes sense and gives you a fighting chance to close a couple of deals to get your business off the ground in a positive way.

That means mail at least 2,500 pieces of mail. What's that going to cost you? Costs vary depending on quantity and type of mailer, but roughly speaking you could probably figure around $0.65-$0.80 would cover a high-quality mailer in that quantity range.

Figure a good list is going to cost you $0.15-$0.20 per name.

Add that up, and worst-case scenario you're looking at roughly $2,500 to mail 2,500 pieces of mail. Of course, you can get things for less money, but I am just making a point in this example.

In this industry, the average wholesale flipper averages around $10,000 profit per deal. I just read an article from a national database company that said in 2017 there were 207,088 homes flipped nationwide with an average fix and flip profit of $68,143. (That is an all-time high.)

So I ask you, even if your first batch of mail did not result in a deal, would you be willing to invest a few batches of mailing to net out over $50,000 on a full fix and flip? Even if you only earn $10,000 on a wholesale flip, would you be willing to invest at least $2,500 to give yourself a chance to earn that $10,000?

Now of course if you ended up with a 2% response, those 2,500 mailers would give you 50 leads, and a much better chance to close at least one deal.

My advice is if you cannot afford to mail at least 2,500 pieces of mail, you should find an alternate means to find deals. You would be better saving your money and spending it on some door hangers and walking door to door to find your first deal. If you don't want to do that, then you might as well give up the whole idea of house flipping because your chances of success are slim at best if you don't give yourself enough leads to work with.

If you're serious about being successful in the REI business, you have to do enough marketing to give yourself enough leads to have something to work with so that you can close deals. If there are no leads, there is nothing to do, and you don't have a business.

Chapter 5

More on Targeting the Perfect Client

Targeting your ideal customer is perhaps the most important thing in marketing.

As I said earlier, you can still get a decent response sending a poor marketing message to a good list. But it is almost impossible to get a good response, no matter how good your marketing message is, to the wrong list. So let's talk about how to identify the best list.

In real estate, there are at least 10 different angles you can take to build your business. You can look for homes that are owned free and clear. You can look for people who are recently divorced. You can look for homes in probate court. You can look for homes owned by a people of a certain age group. You can look for homes that have a certain equity level. You can look for people who are about to lose their house to foreclosure, etc.

Then you also have to decide how you will do business. Will you buy and flip wholesale? Will you buy, fix, and flip wholesale? Will you buy, fix, and flip retail? Do you just want to

assign properties? You get the idea. What you do, and how you plan to do it will have a big impact on the type of list you go for.

Take all these variables into account, and identify what your ideal prospect looks like. And then go about finding the best system to find the lists that come the closest to matching what you're looking for.

It's not rocket science, but if you screw up in this area you can waste a lot of money in mailing to the wrong people. Part of identifying the right people is understanding why people don't buy from you. Once you know that, you can think about the kind of people who will buy from you.

Chapter 6

Why Don't People Buy from You?

Marketing is simple when you boil it down. There are five reasons people will not buy from you:

- They don't have a need for your product.

- They don't have any money.

- They do not need your product right now.

- They don't trust you.

- They are already buying your product from someone else and are happy.

LET'S TALK ABOUT EACH ONE OF THESE AREAS.

They Don't Have A Need For Your Product.

This one is easy. People don't always need what you have to sell. If you are in the real estate business, and you approach someone who loves their house and has no intention of moving, no matter how often or how well you solicit their business, they are going to ignore you.

But that doesn't mean they won't need it in the future sometime!

Timing is everything, but as a small business, you can't afford to market to everyone. This is where targeting the right people is so important. It is vital that you identify people who have the best chance of being interested in your product in the very near future. Those are the people you target. Using software like Find Motivated Sellers Now™ is an excellent tool to narrow your target.

They Don't Have Any Money.

In real estate, the no money argument applies when you're trying to sell the property you already own. The no money argument can be very confusing. Very often, a prospect will use the excuse that they don't have the money. Telling a salesperson you cannot afford something is an easy way to get rid of the pesky salesperson. As a society, we have been trained to do this, because no one likes a pesky salesperson.

But by the same token you need to fish in the pond that has the most fish. In real estate, the right pond is finding people who have a track record of buying investment properties. Getting lists of people who paid cash for homes in the past makes total sense if you're looking for people to pay you cash for your properties. You have to understand, a person like that is an investor, so they're going to be offering you an investor price. But if that works for what you're trying to do, that's a good strategy.

Assuming you are fishing in the right pond, it is extremely important to create a value proposition that will get people to get past the price objection, and see that the value provided is worth the money they pay.

They Don't Need The Product Right Now.

This is an area that you can easily overcome with an effective marketing campaign. Your job is to create a sense of urgency, using deadlines and scarcity, along with repetitive touches, to urge the person to act now versus wait. It is a natural tendency for most

people to procrastinate. By sending a series of regular mailings, showing how the deadline is fast approaching and is about to expire, you can often get someone off their butt to act, when they would've normally done nothing.

Multistep marketing campaigns are extremely effective in overcoming procrastination.

They Don't Trust You.

The fear of loss is one of the strongest motivating factors to do nothing. Fear of loss means people are afraid they're going to be taken. There so many rip-off artists in the world that we are naturally skeptical of anyone that offers something that sounds too good to be true. Your job as a marketer is to alleviate those fears by taking away the risk. There are several methods you can use to take away the risk:

Guarantees of performance

Money-back guarantees

Free trials

Free gifts that they can keep even if they choose to return the product

Testimonials from satisfied customers

Easy communication with your staff

Give something to them before taking their money, and also after. Not just free gifts, but access to you, free advice, extra bonuses that they didn't expect.

They Are Already Buying Your Product Or Service From Someone Else And They Are Happy.

This one seems hard to overcome, but is actually not. In today's world, it is very rare for a company to consistently provide excellent products and services year after year. Even the best suppliers often make mistakes. Or, customers change, and the service provider doesn't change with them. Companies often take their customers for granted, and after a while customers often feel ignored and may be enticed by a new company.

If you've chosen your target market wisely, a person who is happy with someone else might be on your list. Regular marketing to them over a period of time will build your name in their subconscious, and just might give you a shot one day in the future.

Your goal as a marketer is to stay in front of someone often enough that they think of you the next time they're ready to purchase your product or service.

Regular direct mail marketing is a very effective tool for this purpose.

Again, let me use an example in the real estate investing field. As a real estate investor, your goal is to buy properties at a low enough price that you can make a profit after covering all your purchase, repair, and sales costs. Most people do not want to sell their house for a price that is far below the market value. They often don't take into account all the fees, repair costs, etc. that go along with selling through traditional real estate agents. Your challenge as a marketer is to overcome most people's assumption that they need to hire a real estate agent and sell in the traditional manner.

For you to have a chance to get a sale, you need to show the value in what you provide so that accepting an offer far below the market value, without the help of a real estate agent, feels good to the client. You do this by talking about avoiding repair costs, inspections, hassles, real estate fees, holding costs, and pain-and-suffering. You monetize all these issues to show your offer really is not that low when you consider all the factors. These types of things can be done with effective marketing copy.

Another effective method is to be the "Number Two Guy." If a person uses another agent, and they're happy, you don't want to try to tell them that they're not happy. That would only make you look bad and question their decision-making.

Instead congratulate the current agent for doing a good job, and then assure the prospect that if that agent ever stops doing a good job, you'll be ready to step in and take over. This is a longer-term strategy, but can be done effectively with direct mail.

Chapter 7

Mailing List Basics

You can get a good response with a crappy mailer and a good list, but it is impossible to get a good response from a bad list, no matter how good the mailer.

Your mailing list is an extremely important part of your marketing program, especially when you're using direct mail marketing. Once you've identified your ideal customer, it is time to evaluate the different sources to get the data. As I mentioned earlier, since you are getting this book, you already have a relationship with Ken Clothier, and probably own at least one of his mailing list systems. His systems are excellent, and I recommend that is the first place you should look to find your ideal mailing list. However, there are other sources available if you have specialty needs, such as divorces, probates, free and clear, foreclosure, etc. We can help you locate these type of lists if you're interested.

HOW OFTEN IS THE DATA UPDATED?

Reputable companies update their data at least monthly. Ideally, you want a list with extremely fresh data, but that is not always possible based on the source of the data. Many real estate lists that look at property data originate from property tax records. Different municipalities operate on different schedules, and their data can be 6 to 12 months old. However, that may be your only choice.

DOES THE LIST GUARANTEE DELIVERABILITY?

(Deliverability is the ability of the mail piece to be successfully delivered to the prospect.) The answer should be yes, but again, depending on how fresh the data is, this may be impossible to guarantee. A 90% deliverability rating is generally acceptable in the direct mail business. That means up to 10% of the addresses might come back as undeliverable.

10% SEEMS HIGH?

Yes it does, but let me explain why it is so high. All reputable list providers use software programs to Coding Accuracy Support System (CASS) certify, and also run the list through the National Change of Address (NCOA) database to try to ensure the best possible deliverability. Reputable mail houses do the same thing just prior to dropping a mailing. CASS certification looks at the address formatting and ensures that the street, city, state and zip code are properly formatted, and that the address does exist in the postal database. The program will modify the address if possible to make sure it is valid. This program does not check the name against the address, only the address. In other words, we know this is a legitimate house, we just don't know who lives in the house.

NCOA is the database managed by the post office that shows everyone who has moved in the last several years. The post office will forward mail for up to a year if you fill out their postcard and tell them you are moving. After a year, they will no longer forward the mail but the data is included in the NCOA database.

THE PROBLEM IS NOT EVERYONE WHO MOVES INFORMS THE POST OFFICE.

They should, but they don't. You might think it's pretty stupid not to inform the post office you are moving. However, there are a lot of people who are happy to run away from their mail. Maybe bill collectors are chasing them. Or maybe they're just not very organized. If they don't tell the post office they're moving, the post office has no way of adding that data to the NCOA database.

Roughly 7% of the population moves every year. Even if a list company updates its data every month, they have no way of updating it if the people who move don't do their part to inform the system that they have moved.

Not every name is accurate

A secondary issue is that people sometimes use false names to order things, or middle names instead of first names, or purposely misspell names. Data is only as good as its accuracy at the time of input.

Another problem can happen at the point of data entry. If the person entering the data is not careful, names can be butchered. This can cause the mail to be delivered to the wrong place. The homeowner can also reject the mail and return it to the post office, saying it is not his or hers.

Delivery is not accurate

The last thing that happens is that the mailman delivers it to the wrong place. This is more common than you think. Postal carriers often mis-sort a piece of mail and it ends up in the wrong pile. When a letter goes to the wrong house, some people throw it in the trash, and some people return it to the mail driver saying it's not their mail. Rather than trying to deliver it to the proper address, the postman usually just returns it as undeliverable.

Add up all these factors, and you can see why getting a 10% undeliverable rate is not that surprising.

DON'T GET HUNG UP ON UNDELIVERABLE MAIL.

I know it is frustrating when you do a mailing and you get a big pile of undeliverables coming back to you. You feel like you're wasting your money. What really matters is return on investment, not how many undeliverables you get. If your mailing is profitable, don't worry about the undeliverables.

That doesn't mean you have to be stupid with your money either. If you plan to use the list more than once, take the time to go through the list and delete all of the undeliverables prior to doing a second mailing. This way you won't repeat the problem. Managing and cleaning up your list is also a smart thing to do in your overall marketing program.

TURN YOUR UNDELIVERABLE MAIL INTO SUPER HOT LEADS

One thing you can do that few investors think about is to hire a skip tracing service to track down your undeliverable mail. Why would you do that? Because when something is undeliverable that means that for some reason name you have is the property owner is either not correct or something went wrong with the address. In most cases, you bought your list, and that list came from property tax data. That means that they had incorrect information in the property tax records. The person that owns that property is not getting his mail.

Think about what that means. It means that there's a good chance the property is vacant. It also means is a good chance the owner may not be paying his property taxes. There's a good chance the property is a pain in the butt to the owner and he would not mind getting rid of it. The fact is that undeliverable mail you can skip trace can often be some of the best leads you can find.

CAN I USE A LIST OVER AND OVER AGAIN?

Different list companies have different policies. Most companies that are in the list business will have two different rates. They will have a one-time use rate and an unlimited use rate. Typically the unlimited use cost is about 50% higher than the one-time use cost. Most major list compilers do charge for unlimited use. If a list broker tells you something different, be a little suspicious and dig more to find out where he or she is getting the list.

There are private list sources that may only charge you one fee no matter if it's a single use or multiple uses. It is very important that you clarify this prior to buying a list. You can get into trouble if you violate the policy.

Don't get hung up on the cost of the list. Just like identifying your ideal prospect is critical to your success, getting a list of those prospects is equally critical. Paying a few pennies more for a good list will pay for itself many times over. Too many people make the mistake of going for the low bid list, only to be disappointed to find out it was garbage. Remember, the list will be the least expensive part of your marketing campaign, even if you pay a premium price for it. Don't be a cheapskate when it comes to buying lists.

Chapter 8

Increasing Results

It doesn't matter what you think or what I think about a mailer design. All that matters is what the market thinks.

PROFIT RESULTS MATTER, <u>NOT</u> RESPONSE RATES

One of the biggest mistakes marketers make, especially in the direct-mail world, is getting hung up on percent response rates versus return on investment. I can't tell you how many times I've been asked, "What kind of response rate can I expect to get on this mailing?" Although it is a practical question, it is only one part of the question they should be asking. The second is, "What is your typical closing rate on a lead, and how much money do you make on a typical deal?"

There is no average response rate. That number does not exist. Response rates can be anywhere from zero to as high as 100%. Yes, it is true that most mailings do fall into the

lower end of that spectrum, and it is not unusual to get less than a 2% response on a mailing. But there's still no average.

There are so many factors that affect response rate that is not possible to boil it all down to an average. The quality of the list, the quality of the mail piece, timeliness, whether or not the mail piece has the proper offer, call to action, and guarantee are all factors that play into the response rate. Quantity of mail piece has a huge impact as well. The smaller your mailing, the harder it is to get averages that make statistical sense. If you only mail 250 pieces of mail every month for a year, it would not be surprising to get zero response on one mailing and 25 responses on the next. You need at least 5,000 mailers to be able to get an average that means anything.

The best thing you can do is to track a cumulative response rate when you're dealing with a lot of small mailings. As you get a statistically valid number, then you can start to test other mail pieces against that to see if you can improve on the numbers.

Another huge factor that affects response rates is your objective. Asking for someone to call you for more information, or to respond for a free report, is a lot easier than trying to make an actual sale with your mail piece. In addition, the higher the price, the lower the response rates tend to be.

Here's a rule of thumb. If you're trying to make a sale with your mail piece, and you're going to cold prospects, keep the offer under $100 for the best results. Once they have made that initial purchase, then you can upsell them on more expensive offers. If you're selling to existing clients, your offer can range from $79 to $800. Anything over $800 normally requires some sort of personal contact in addition to the mail piece. If you try to sell items higher than $800 you're going to find it extremely difficult to sell in a one-step mailing. For real estate investors, almost all of your prospects will require a personal conversation to turn into a sale.

LET'S GET BACK TO RESULTS.

I'm not saying not to worry about your response rates, but the other two factors are equally, if not more, important. It is those three factors combined together, along with considering the cost of the marketing program, that allow you to calculate the return on investment.

Let's say you mail 1,000 pieces of mail, and receive a 2% response rate, which consisted of people interested in your service. Let's also assume your typical sale nets you $10,000

profit. I'm also going to assume that for every 10 leads you get, you typically close one of those deals.

If you get a 2% response rate on 1,000 pieces of mail, that is 20 leads. If you can close 10% of those leads, that is two deals. If you make $10,000 per deal, that is $20,000 profit you made on this campaign. If you spent $1,000 on the campaign and you earned $20,000 profit, that is a 20 to 1 return on investment. I think just about anyone would repeat that campaign with those kinds of numbers. Now, let's assume you had a seven-step mailing campaign, and over the seven mailers, you got a grand total of 4% response. Let's assume each mailer cost you $1000, so you spent $7,000 total on your mail campaign. Your 4% response was 40 leads, and your 10% closing ratio netted you four deals, or $40,000. Your return on investment was $40,000/$7,000=5.7 times money spent. Would you repeat that mailing?

Now let's take that same example and assume you only got a 2% response rate total from all 7 mailings, but you still got a 10% closing rate and still made $10,000 per deal. That would be 20 leads with one deal, earning you $20,000. The mail piece still cost you $7,000 so you still made a $20,000/$7,000 = 2.8 to 1 return on investment. Still an excellent return.

Now let's look at this another way. Instead of focusing so much on response rates, let's focus on increasing your closing ratio. If you could take your closing ratio from 10% to 20%, you can double your profits with the same number of leads. How much would you be willing to spend on the 20 leads you have, to increase your closing ratio from 2 to 4 on the 20? It's a lot easier to improve closing rates than it is to increase response rates.

LIFETIME VALUE OF THE CUSTOMER IS A HUGE FACTOR TO CONSIDER.

Spending more money than you take in on the initial campaign is not necessarily a bad thing. If the lifetime value of your customer provides an adequate rate of return, it still may make sense to do a marketing campaign, even though the initial numbers may not be all that exciting.

Let's say that on the initial sale, you only make $1,000 for your product or service. However, a good customer will spend $1,000 per year with you. Let's also say that a typical customer stays with you for five years. The lifetime value of a customer in this scenario is 5 × $1,000, or $5,000.

You might not see how this applies in real estate. Consider this: We have one client who did 10 different mailings of 1,000 pieces of mail. That's all he has ever done, and

he started two years ago. The first deal he made was with an investor who sold him 10 houses at one time. The same investor led him to another investor with whom he was able to make a deal for over 300 houses. He now has a portfolio of 350 houses that came from 10 – 1,000 piece postcard mailings. I can't even figure that return on investment it is so high.

If your initial mailing campaign cost $1,000 and you only make $1,000 on the first deal, that can still be a good thing when considering lifetime value.

THE BIGGEST CHALLENGE FOR REIs IS COMPETITION FROM OTHER REIs

One of the biggest things REIs miss when considering what they need to do to find and close more deals is the reality of competition in the marketplace. I am always hearing from people in the industry that response rates for almost every type of marketing medium are going down, down, down.

The mistake they make is thinking that the methods are not working.

That is where they are wrong. I will specifically address direct mail here since that is my primary focus in this book, but this concept applies to all marketing methods.

The problem is not that there are fewer deals to be had or that direct mail doesn't work anymore. The problem is that the number of REIs is growing at a fast pace. Have you noticed all the TV shows that focus on house flipping? Have you noticed you see more and more advertisements on radio, TV and in the mail from "gurus" who are hosting seminars on how to flip houses and get rich?

The fact is that all this attention on house flipping has the number of new REIs entering the marketplace growing at a breakneck pace. Moreover, every one of these "gurus" is teaching that you need to spend money on marketing to find leads that you can hopefully turn into deals that are worth tens of thousands of dollars in profit. They are also teaching the seminar goers how to target "prime prospects." Just about every teacher says to go after properties that have high equity, fit into price ranges of zero to $200,000, and have absentee owners. Additionally, they will teach you to go after probate leads or pre-foreclosure leads.

It is simple math that if you add more and more competitors to any market, each one of them is going to get a smaller share of the leads and deals. You see, there is a finite number of deals to be had in any marketplace. Even if most of the newcomers will likely not last and go away, they are still marketing through the mail. They may not know what

they are doing, but they can pay someone like me to mail postcards or letters telling the homeowner that they want to buy their house. Even a blind squirrel occasionally finds an acorn.

However, what they miss is that by using the cheapest methods, often the response is compromised. With all the competition, it is not enough to merely put the most inexpensive piece of mail out in the marketplace. You need to mail the most effective piece – even if it costs more.

Where a few years ago, a property owner who owned a property that fit into the high equity and absentee owner range might get a letter or postcard from one person occasionally, those same prospects are getting solicitations by mail, cold calls, text, Google and Facebook retargeting, and other methods every week. I own properties that fit this scenario, and there is not a week that goes by that I do not get at least five mailers, a couple of cold phone calls, and I am starting to get unsolicited texts (which is illegal).

Even if you are excellent, some of the deals are going to go to the rookies out of pure luck. That means fewer deals for you.

The bottom line is the competition is fierce.

THAT'S WHERE YOU, AS AN INVESTOR AND MARKETER, NEED TO STEP UP YOUR GAME.

It is no longer enough to use a simple postcard, or yellow letter, especially the same designs that everyone else is using. You need to get creative and think about how you can stand out above the competition, so they call you instead of them.

If you are smart about how you market to the prospects, such as hitting them more than once, and being unique in your mailers, you can reduce your list spend and also improve both front-end and back-end results.

If you focus on buying quality lists, and doing quality mailers that do convert, yes, you will spend more money. But not a lot more. However, your results concerning lead generation and deal closing will likely be a lot better.

Here is the good news. First, because there is such a high upside to buying and selling houses, there is plenty of profit to allow you to spend more to get leads. You can still make a good living doing this even with all the competition.

The second bit of good news is that most of your competitors will mail one time and never mail again. They don't understand what it takes to succeed in REI marketing, and they will not invest enough money in marketing to give themselves a chance to succeed. Statistics show that 80% of the deals are being done by 20% of the REIs. The newcomers will spend some money, not get enough leads to close a deal, and then decide this business is not good and go away. Granted, there will be another newcomer to take their place tomorrow, but a tiny percentage will succeed and end up being a long-term competitor to you.

However, it is still vital that you step up your game.

THE SOLUTION TO FIERCE COMPETITION:

Be Unique

Be Frequent

That's right. You have to be unique and frequent to win the lead game.

When I say unique, that means you have to use mailers that are unique and different that stand out from the crowd. You want your stuff to be something the prospect keeps, even if he or she is not ready to call you today. You want yours to be the one that does not get thrown in the trash.

When I say frequent, I am talking about mailing to the same lead more than one time. There are different philosophies as to how many times and how close together the mailers should hit. But every successful marketer agrees that frequency is a crucial element to success in any market, but especially the REI market.

If your stuff is unique and then on top of that, you hit the same prospect multiple times, there is a good chance that they will start to remember you over all the others who send the same old cheap postcards one time each and are gone.

There is an adage in direct mail that says you should keep mailing to the same list, over and over, until that list stops performing. That could be three times. It could be six times. It could be 20 times. Don't try to guess. Let the market decide. Just keep mailing until your ROI stops being acceptable.

HOW CLOSE TOGETHER SHOULD THE MAILERS BE?

There are two primary schools of thought on that topic. The answer depends on your strategy. One strategy is to hit a lead often and close together so that you can catch those who are currently considering selling their house. I have clients who mail as many as seven times within 30 days to the same prospect. In doing this, they are making a statement to the prospects that they are serious about buying their house and the multi-touch approach does garner attention.

Some people mail every ten days for 3 to 5 touches. There too are looking for those people who are ready to sell now, but just spread out their mail a bit more.

Then some people take more of a long-term approach and mail once a month for a full year to the same leads. The philosophy here is to try to build more of a long-term brand and catch those people who are both ready now and also the others who may be prepared in the near-term future of 6-12 months. I have clients who have closed deals from people who got their mailers over and over and actually saved a pile of them and called as much as two years later to offer to sell their house. The multi-touch approach built the brand enough that the prospect chose to save their stuff and eventually call.

Plus, there is another factor to consider. Direct mail response rates in the REI industry range from .2% (2 leads out of 1,000 mailers) to about 4% (40 leads out of 1,000 mailers). Most of the campaigns we see from people that use our strategies and mailers are in the 1%-1.5% range, with an occasional spike to up to 4%.

All too often, real estate investors will buy a mailing list, mail to it one time, get whatever response they get, and then conclude they need to buy another list to get some more leads.

THEY ARE MAKING A HUGE MISTAKE.

The fact is that in the industry, a 1% to 2% response rate is very common. That means that 98% to 99% did not respond. However, just because they didn't respond now doesn't mean they weren't interested. There are many reasons people don't respond, and only one of those is lack of interest.

But that does not mean they wouldn't respond in the future. Let's look at some of the reasons people don't respond.

1) They didn't see the mailer because it did not stand out in the pile of mail.

2) They didn't pick up the mail – someone else did, and they chose to throw it away without even paying attention to the offer.

3) It didn't get to the recipient (the mail service in the US is not perfect, and they deliver to the wrong address at times).

4) They saw the mailer, but it didn't get their attention because the headline was not compelling.

5) They saw it, but were too busy to respond and then forgot about it later.

6) They saw it, saved it to respond later, but lost it in their pile of mail on their desk.

7) The saw it, were not interested today, but saved it because they thought they might be interested later.

8) They were on vacation, and when they got back, they had a massive pile of mail, and due to pure information overload, they didn't notice it and threw it away.

9) The information on the list was incorrect and the mail was returned.

I am sure there are more reasons to add to this list. The point is if you only mail once, you are missing the chance to hit people who may have missed it for any of these reasons.

The smart move is to go after the 98% to 99% who did not respond a few more times to at least give yourself a chance for every prospect to see, read, and respond if they are interested.

LET'S GET BACK TO THE "BEING UNIQUE" CONCEPT.

Earlier, when I said that I get a pile of mailers every single week from REIs wanting to buy my houses, what I didn't mention is almost all of them are small postcards – printed as cheaply as possible. I get really crappy letters that look like they were mass produced on a copier. None of them stand out. It just looks like junk mail, and I toss it in the trash.

NOTHING IS MEMORABLE, SO NO ONE STANDS OUT.

Every once in a while, I get a mailer that does stand out, and I save it. Now for me, I am keeping it because I am in the direct mail business and I use these for ideas for to further develop my line of unique mailers. Plus, I not only look at REI mailers, but mailers from all different industries and see how I can apply some of the better concepts to this industry.

WHAT TYPES OF THINGS CAN YOU DO TO STAND OUT?

Of course, some of the basics, which I have already covered in other parts of this book, are to make things look as personal as possible. Use handwritten fonts. Use real stamps. Use unique envelopes that seem important.

However, you can do more. Make your mailer larger than a standard letter or postcard size. Make it look like a critical document such as some notice from the bank or government agency. You can add a photo of the prospect's house to the front of a postcard or letter. You can use a unique method of response such as a text response. You can make an exclusive offer that is different from your competition. Some examples of very effective and unique mailers that I designed are below.

Accupix™

Ability to Respond by Text   *Handwritten*

Unique Letters

Cards

Outside   ### Inside

Giant Size Mailers

Inside   ### Outside

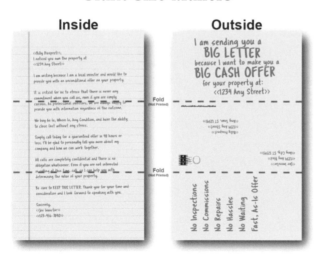

Pressure Seal Self-Mailer

FRONT   ### INSIDE

ADD THE NEWEST TECHNOLOGY TO YOUR MAILERS AND WATCH THE RESPONSE RATES GO UP!

I talk about being unique so that your mailers stand out from your competition; one way to do that is to work with a direct mail company who is continually developing new and innovative mailers.

At this point, I'm going to take credit for a couple of innovations that I created.

The first is what I call Accupix Mailers™. We developed the technology to be able to take your mailing list, and upload it to a program that we wrote, and pull the Google Street View image of each house on the mailing list (if an image exists). We can then mail merge that into any mailer, be it postcards, letters, or self-mailers.

We introduced this in late 2017, and have seen excellent results concerning response rates. We were the first to introduce this to the market, and as of the date of this writing, there is only one other mailing company in the US that offers the service. Note: Google does charge a fee for each image that you download, which is built into our pricing.

The reason it works is straightforward. When people are looking through their mail, often over the trash can, you have one to three seconds to get their attention. If someone is flipping through his or her mail, and he or she sees a picture of his or her own house, don't you think he or she might at least take a second look?

The fact is they do take a second look, and they often save the mailer with intent to respond either immediately or sometime later.

Note that when using this technology, roughly about 10% of the properties will not have images. Make sure that the company you use has a solution to handle that situation. Make sure they are not mailing postcards or letters with blank images. Also, make sure they are not deleting those records from the database and not mailing to them. If they are doing that, they owe you a credit.

Our solution is to substitute a generic picture for all the records that do not have a Google image so that the entire database still gets mailed.

ADD A TEXT RESPONSE OPTION AND WATCH YOUR RESPONSE RATES GO UP EVEN MORE

In June 2018, we introduced a second innovation that is unique to the REI industry. We call it Accutxt™.

We have partnered with a technology provider that can add a text response mechanism to any direct mail piece. This system is one-of-a-kind, and currently, we are the only company offering this to the REI industry in the nation. It is a straightforward but effective concept. We add the option on the mail piece to respond by text to your offer. They still have the option to call a phone number as well.

When they do respond, they get instant text response that is fully personalized and tied to the database.

If you look at the postcard below, you'll see an example of what I'm talking about.

In this case, the outgoing offer is "text for an instant cash offer." You will also notice, that we have combined our AccuPix™ product with the AccuTxt™ product for a super powerful combination.

We call this gcPowerMail™.

HE WHO SPENDS THE MOST TO GET A LEAD WINS THE GAME

That's right, he who is willing to spend the most to acquire and close a lead usually wins the game. But that is not what most REIs do. They usually go the other direction.

There is a reason why most REIs go with the cheapest mailer they can find, which is usually a small postcard. It is because they are trying to keep their marketing cost low. Of course, it is good business to control your costs. However, what they miss is that by using the cheapest methods, often the response is compromised. With all the competition, it is not enough to merely put the cheapest piece of mail out in the marketplace. You need to mail the most effective piece – even if it costs more.

I cannot stress this point enough. You will recover the incremental cost of more expensive, but effective mailers many times over with increased profits that the mailers generate.

Let me give you an illustration

Let's say that your "cheap" mailer costs you $.45 each to mail, and it brings you a .5% response rate (5 leads for every 1,000 mailers).

Let's also assume that you make $10,000 profit on every deal you close, and it takes you 25 leads to close one deal (4% closing rate which is typical in the market).

Let's also say you mail 5,000 mailers one time to each lead.

Doing the math on this, here is how it shakes out:

5,000 leads bought at $.10 each = $500 for mailing list

5,000 mailers x $.45 each = $2,250 spent on mail.

Total Mail spend = $2,750

At .5% response, you get 25 leads from this mailer (5,000 x .005 = 25). Since it takes you 25 leads to close a deal, you close one deal and make $10,000 profit.

ROI

$2,750 spent on mail

$10,000 earned in profit

$7,250 net profit. Pretty good.

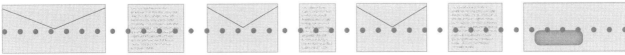

Now let's look at the same example, except you choose to mail something that is unique and memorable, but costs more.

Plus, you also brought a better list, but that also costs more. However, because the list and mailer are better, it generates a better response. Let's assume you spend 50% more on both lists and the mailers. Let's say it gets you 1% response, which is double what you got from the cheaper mailers.

Doing the math on this, here is how it shakes out:

5,000 leads bought at $.15 each = $750 for mailing list

5,000 mailers x $.67 each = $3,350 spent on mail.

Total Mail spend = $4,100

However, now you have 50 leads instead of 25 (1% of 5,000 is 50).

Using the same closing rate of 1 in 25, you now close two deals instead of one.

That brings in $20,000 cash.

You spent $4,100 on the list plus mailing, so your net profit is $15,900 net profit. **More than double what you made before, even though you spent more on mail.**

The reason is the response rate. Spending a little more to get better leads and better response rate easily pays for itself plus a lot more profit.

So spending 50% more on list and mail cost, which doubled your response rate up front, resulted in $15,900 in net profit versus $7,250 net profit in the original example. That is more than double the profit.

Makes sense...right?

INCREASING THE BACK-END RESPONSE INCREASES PROFITS EXPONENTIALLY

Another colossal mistake REIs make is not accepting the fact that they are in sales and embracing the process of converting a lead into a deal. Since I have been in sales for over 30 years, I feel qualified to address this point.

I have always said "the fortune is in the follow-up," and that is also true in this market.

What if you could improve your back-end closing rate for deals also? What do you think that would do to your profit numbers? Of course, they will go up, but I bet you don't

realize just how much a small increase in front-end response rates and back-end deal closing rates can exponentially increase profits.

A typical REI will spend a bunch of money on marketing, generate some leads, and then do a poor job of converting those leads. They often will drop the ball in many ways. They don't call the lead promptly after the prospect responds. If they don't talk to them live, they often do not follow up with additional calls until they do reach the prospect live. They usually will have one conversation, and if that conversation does not immediately turn into a "hot lead," they put it on the back burner and often forget about it. They don't have any printed follow-up material to send. Often they do not even own business cards.

ON THE BACK-END, THE FORMULA IS THE SAME FOR INCREASING YOUR CLOSING RATIO.

Be Frequent

Be Unique

It merely means you have to do more than your competition to win the deals. People don't usually make instant decisions when it comes to selling their house. Often it takes months for them to make a decision. The person who is in their face the most is likely to get the deal when they finally make a decision. Hit them often with phone calls, emails, direct mail, and texts. Do something different than most people would do to stand out.

If you are not aggressively and repeatedly marketing to each lead that you generate from your direct mail, you're leaving a tremendous amount of money on the table.

A simple step is to get some letterhead and a nice brochure printed that you can mail to each prospect. Get some business cards and give them out. Also sign up for a cheap email autoresponder service, such as MailChimp, and start sending the prospect a series of automatic emails over the next year to keep your name in front of them.

We have clients who close as many as one out of 10 leads using this type of strategy. Imagine how much more money you would see if instead of one out of 25, you could close one out of 10? Yes, it might cost you some money on follow-up to get these results, but it is chump-change as compared to how much more you could make.

Again, using a specific example with real numbers will explain this very clearly as to how much it can be worth you with only a small increase in closing rate.

Let's go back to our original example. Remember you mailed 5,000 leads and got a .5% response. That gave you 25 leads from this mailer. Since it takes you 25 leads to close a deal, you close one deal and make $10,000 profit. After you factor in the mailing cost, your net profit is $7,250.

Remember, by spending a little more to get a better list and better mailer, you increased your response rate to 1.0% response, and got 50 leads from this mailer. With the old way of follow up, it still takes you 25 leads to close a deal, you close two deals and make $20,000 profit, and a $15,900 net after mail cost. It was better than the initial example, but there is a lot more money to be had.

NOW LET'S LOOK AT WHAT INCREASING YOUR BACK-END CLOSING RATE CAN MEAN IN REAL MONEY.

Let's assume that you increase your back-end marketing effort and spend $50 per lead to do various marketing initiatives. You might send them a letter every month, do some emailing, some calling, and then send them a couple of nice "shock-and-awe" packages. (A shock and awe package is a box of goodies that someone will notice and love.) Let's assume this effort results in you going from one in 25 leads closed to one in 16. That is taking you form a 4% closing rate to 6%. Not a massive jump, but it is significant in terms of money in your pocket.

50 leads x $50 = $2,500 spent in follow-up marketing.

50 leads/16 = 3 deals closed the new way. Profit = $30,000 - $2,500 spent on marketing - $4,100 spent on original mail cost = $23,400 profit.

Now, you spent a little more on mail, $4,100, but got a better response rate of 1%, and you did a better job of closing deals, improving your deal-closing results to one in 16 leads. The result was a net profit of $23,400! That is almost four times better profit than where you started, with only slightly better lead generation and closing rate results.

> **The increase in profits is exponential when you focus on better front-end and also back-end results.**

NOW LET'S DREAM A LITTLE...

Let's say that instead of mailing 5,000, you increased your list to 20,000, and you hit each name on that list three times. That is a total of 60,000 mailers. (You are hitting them three

times to help with your brand recognition, which will help response rates and closing rates on the back-end.)

Let's use our same example as above, with the second scenario where you spend more on the mailers and list, but get more leads. We will also assume that you are going to focus on back-end closing and you can generate a closing ratio of 1 in 16 leads.

Let's say that your "cheap" mailer costs you $.45 each to mail, and it brings you a .5% response rate (5 leads for every 1,000 mailers).

THE "CHEAP WAY"

List cost: 60,000 x $.10 each = $6,000 (we hit each name only one time)

Mailer Cost: 60,000 x $.45 each = $27,000

Total Mailing cost + List: 33,000

Response rate .5% = 60,000 x .5% = 300 Leads

Closing Rate 1 in 25 = 300/25 = 12 deals

Profit of $10,000 per deal x 12 deals = $120,000 cash in.

Net Profit $120,000 - $33,000 mail cost = $87,000 Profit.

That is a decent profit, **but it could be a whole lot better**.

NOW LET'S LOOK AT DOING IT THE "SMART" WAY

List cost: 20,000 x $.15 each = $3,000 (we hit the same list 3 times)

Mailer Cost: 60,000 x $.67 each = $40,200

Total Mailing cost + List: $43,200

Response rate 1% = 60,000 x 1% = 600 Leads

Closing Rate 1 in 16 = 600/16 = 37 deals

Back-end marketing spend to close deals = $50 per lead x 600 = $30,000

Profit of $10,000 per deal x 37 deals = $370,000 cash in.

Net Profit $370,000 - $43,200 mail cost - $30,000 back-end marketing cost = $296,800 Profit.

WHICH SOUNDS BETTER? $296,800 OR $87,000?

Now, of course, these are just what-if scenarios. However, even if you cut the results in half on the $296,800 scenario, you are still way better off.

In conclusion, the answer to exponential improvements in your net profit does not lie in cutting costs on direct mail. The answer lies in finding more effective mailers, and at the same time focusing on working leads you do get to the best of your ability. Spending more money to get better lists and more effective mailers, and spending more money than your competitors to close the deals will result in dramatic increases in your net profits.

USING OFFLINE TO PROMOTE ONLINE AND VICE-VERSA

One of the most powerful marketing strategies you can use is to combine offline direct mail marketing with online marketing. In online marketing, you place ads or send emails directing people to a landing page, opt-in page, or squeeze page on a website. (Landing pages, opt-in pages, and squeeze pages are all terms for a webpage that forces the visitor to fill something out to get further information or move to the next step.) Once the person fills out the information on the landing or squeeze page, they are entered into an email auto-responder series and sales funnel.

The same thing can be done with direct mail. Initially send out a mail piece that drives a person to an online landing page or squeeze page, and the online sales funnel takes over from there. If you already have an online system that has numbers that will work financially, it is extremely easy to also make that work offline. The beauty of this is it expands your prospect base. It also brings in a whole new element of potential customers who may not be people you could find online.

There are several different ways you can choose to market combining direct mail with online marketing. One option is to use your direct mail campaign to drive people to an opt-in page where your sole objective is to get the prospect to give you their name and email. The prospect will then be entered into an auto-responder series through which you present your product or service. At the same time, the prospect will be redirected to a webpage, the next step in your sales funnel. It is extremely important to offer the prospect something of value in exchange for opting in. It can be a free special report, book, newsletter, or other offer that is compelling.

Postcards or short letters are used for this type of marketing. The postcard's job is to drive someone to the webpage, and let the webpage do the selling. Typically the postcard will have a headline, an irresistible offer which will get them to the webpage, and then a

call to action with instructions. Often there is an option to either make a phone call, or go to a webpage.

ADD AN ONLINE KICKER TO INCREASE RESPONSE RATES EVEN MORE

We have been speaking about using offline tools to drive online marketing. We can kick this up a notch with this simple trick. Technically we are focusing on the online portion of the strategy, but it is especially attractive when using direct mail to drive traffic.

One of the latest and most effective online techniques, used by more and more marketers, is the use of re-marketing or re-targeting ads. These are ads from Google that will follow an online user from one website to another.

Let me explain. Let's say you send out a direct mail piece, and direct a person to a landing page. At that point, the person has the choice of filling out the opt-in box on that page, or just going to another website. Most people will move on without filling out the opt-in box. In the past, there was no way to capture that lead. If they went away without opting in, they were lost forever.

Not anymore.

Using re-targeting technology, the system will apply cookies or pixels to the computer of the visitor. Those cookies will follow them to whatever website they visit. Attached to those cookies are ads for your particular product or service. When the person goes to other websites that allow these types of ads, the ads will pop up on their screen. They call that 'impressions.' One extremely effective way to boost your response rates of any marketing campaign, online or offline, is to utilize this re-marketing technology. These ads will follow the user around for as long as you are willing to pay.

The benefit is twofold. First, the cost of these ads is relatively inexpensive, and there are systems out there that automate this process and make it very simple. Graphic Connections Group has one of those systems. Second, this gives you a much greater chance of getting the prospect's attention, as they will be hit multiple times with your offer. It's no longer over if they leave your website without opting in.

This is one of the most powerful technologies available online today. Combining that with a direct mail campaign can dramatically increase the response rates of your campaign.

Chapter 9

Types of Direct Mail

*With all the competition in the REI market,
being unique is extremely critical
to success.*

TYPES OF DIRECT MAIL

Format is very important in direct mail. When talking about format, I mean what the mail piece looks like. Different formats have different purposes.

THE RULE OF 3-30

The second most common thing everybody does at the end of the day is go to the pile of mail. The first is going to the bathroom. When you arrive home every day to get your big pile of mail that's waiting in your mailbox, most people sort through it quickly and decide

what they're going to keep and what they're going to throw in the trash. They often sort right over the trashcan.

Typically, people will take three seconds to decide if they're going to keep the mail or throw it away. And then they take 30 seconds to decide if they're going to look more carefully at your particular mail piece. Thus you have the rule of 3-30.

The format of your direct mail piece can dramatically impact whether you pass the 3-30 test.

For the purposes of our discussion, we will focus on five main types of direct mail used in the real estate market: postcards, letters, self-mailers, priority or special delivery mail, and Lumpy Mail.

Each of these types of mail has its place, depending on the strategy you're trying to implement.

POSTCARDS

The post office's definition of a postcard is a single sheet of thick cardstock paper, ranging in size from 3.5 x 5 inches to 4.25 x 6 inches. It can be printed in full color on both sides, black and white on both sides, or a combination of the two. The design can be simple type in black and white, full-color with pictures, or anything in between.

It is also common to see postcards much larger than that. You'll see them as large as 5.5 x 11" in your mailbox. In fact, with the advent of Every Door Direct Mail®, you'll even see sizes as large as 10 x 13". However, when you have a postcard larger than 4.25 x 6", you get kicked up into the "letter" category for postage. For the purposes of our discussion, we will use the term postcard for all single sheet mailers no matter what the size. Just keep in mind as your postcards get larger, the postage gets more expensive.

Let me also say that in general marketing, direct mail is often used to actually sell a product right from the mailer. That never happens in real estate. Because the transactions are so large, you must have a conversation with the prospect before you can ever make a sale. Because of that, all real estate marketing has the intention of generating a lead in the form of a phone call, an email, or website visit.

There are 3 primary sizes of postcards that get used in the direct mail business. Small (4.25 x 5.5"), Large (5.5 x 8.5"), and Oversized (5.5 x 11").

Small
4.25" × 5.25"

Oversized
5.5" × 11"

Large
5.55" × 8.5"

It is up to the person sending the postcard to handle responses in a way that leads to sales. In general, the larger the postcard, the better the response. Why is this? If you go back a few paragraphs, you'll note that I talked about how many people will sort their mail over the trashcan. As they are sorting the mail over the trashcan, the items that are bigger naturally stand out. An oversized postcard that is 5.5 x 11" definitely stands out in the mail. It allows you a better chance to get someone's attention before they throw it away.

It is possible to have a longer sales message on the larger postcards, which gives you a chance to stand out from your competition.

As a general rule, larger postcards "pull," or perform, better than smaller postcards. The only exception to that is two mail drops of small postcards will out-pull one large postcard drop. However, if you go to two mail drops of large postcards, it will out-pull two mail drops of small postcards.

The benefit to using postcards is that the recipient can see the marketing message without having to open an envelope. There are many marketers who believe this makes them extremely effective.

Fancy designs are not always necessary to get a good postcard response.

In the real estate business, we have found that the simple, clearly worded postcards seem to pull better than postcards with fancy graphics. We have had especially good success with postcards that look like an important notice, or those that look handwritten.

The only way to really find out what works for you is to test.

SELF-MAILERS

Self-mailers consist of a piece of paper that is folded, and usually tabbed, and is mailed without an envelope. It can be on thin paper or card stock.

The advantage of self-mailers is that you avoid the cost of an envelope, and the cost of stuffing the mail into an envelope. Typically, this means the mail is a little cheaper. You can do some fairly creative things with self-mailers, and they usually will get opened if done correctly. A disadvantage is that it is easy for self-mailers to get chewed up in the mail.

With the self-mailer, you can add teaser copy on the outside, or make it look very personal like a handwritten note or invitation. Your imagination is the limit.

LETTERS

Letters consist of a piece of paper with either a handwritten or typed message, folded into an envelope. You can use varying sizes of envelopes.

There are two schools of thought in letter mailing. The first is trying to make the envelope look like a personal letter from a friend or family member, using things like handwritten fonts, live stamps, applied return address labels, blue or red ink, invitation style envelopes, or colored envelopes. These techniques all help to make things look more personal. The job of the envelope is to get the person to open it. That's it. Once the person opens the envelope, it has done its job and the focus is on what is inside.

The second school of thought is to make the envelope look like it contains something extremely important. You could even make it look like it came from a bank or the IRS. Sometimes using a window envelope makes it look official as well. There are all kinds of strategies used to make things look important.

A third strategy is to use teaser copy on the outside of the envelope. Teaser copy is printing on the outside of the envelope, whose goal it is to get the person to open the envelope and look inside. This method is a bit more challenging, because if your teaser copy is not particularly compelling, the envelope will likely go straight to the trash. Most people do not like to read obvious junk mail. Envelopes with teaser copy are usually obvious junk mail. We very rarely see anyone using teaser copy in the real estate market. In most cases, it is not proven to be very effective.

In general, I prefer to use the personalized approach in most cases. Our clients use two main types of letter mailers. One is a handwritten yellow letter, with a handwritten font on the outside envelope. The other is a typed business letter with a business font on the envelope.

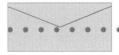

PRIORITY/SPECIAL DELIVERY MAIL

Here we are talking about envelopes that stand out above and beyond normal plain envelopes. Examples are FedEx overnight envelopes, UPS Next Day Air, or simulated envelopes that are made to look like they contain important documents. Usually these envelopes are made of thicker paper stock, or cardboard, and/or at least 6 x 9 inches in size.

There is no question these type of envelopes get opened. It is a rare person that is going to throw away an envelope like this without at least checking out what's inside first. The drawback is that if you go larger than 6 x 9, the postage is quite a bit more for these types of envelopes. In some special cases, we have had clients use actual FedEx or UPS

overnight envelopes, and use those services to also deliver the mail. They spent between $7 and $30 per envelope for the mail piece. In those cases, they had a very exclusive list of high-end properties, and the potential profit was large enough to justify the expenditure.

You can guarantee, if you send a mailer via FedEx, the person on the other end is going to pay attention to what's in the envelope.

Many companies, including mine, have designed envelopes to simulate these overnight envelopes, but are far cheaper to mail. In addition, we have developed standard mail postage methods, which allow us to spend far less money on postage on these larger envelopes. However, even with all those strategies in place, they are still more expensive to mail than postcards or standard sized letters.

Remember, the job of the envelope is to get the customer to open the mail. Once it is open, it is the contents inside that take center stage. So no matter what type of envelope you use, you'd better have an offer that is irresistible and will lead you to some very profitable sales.

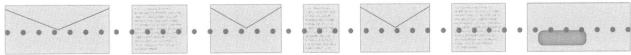

LUMPY MAIL

Lumpy Mail is mail that has some bulk to it. There are all kinds of unusual items that you can mail. It might be a bank bag that has a letter inside. It might be a large poster rolled up in a tube, a Frisbee with a message on it, a small trash can with a sales letter crumpled up inside, or any other creative thing you can think of.

I mentioned earlier that it's possible to get a 100% response rate. A man named John Goldman mailed a watermelon through the mail to a hand-selected mailing list. He literally put stamps on an actual watermelon, taped a mailing label to it, and mailed it through the US mail. They accepted it and delivered it. 100% of the recipients who received that watermelon took the action that John requested.

It worked because it was so outrageous that the people getting it could not help but respond.

The benefit of Lumpy Mail is that it gets opened 100% of the time. There is no way a person is going to receive a piece of Lumpy Mail and ignore it. It gets noticed because it naturally has to be on the top of the mail pile just because it's lumpy.

There's no question that Lumpy Mail costs more to send. But again, as I mentioned before in this book, you cannot just focus on one aspect of the project. You have to focus on the return on investment.

I have another example of a Lumpy Mail piece to illustrate this point. I recently received a FedEx envelope in the mail. Inside was an item that was about a half inch thick, and the size of a small book. When I opened the cover, a video automatically started playing with an offer. It was so cool I watched the entire six minute video. This particular offer was an invitation to attend a very high-end networking or "mastermind" group, and the price was $1,000. The initial video asked me to call them, which I did. I spoke to a salesman, who easily talked me into the $1,000 price point. He also told me that if I was happy with the mastermind group, the ultimate price would be $10,000.

I accepted his offer, attended the meeting, liked it, and ended up spending the $10,000. This particular group was focused on marketing, and the leader used this example as part

of our discussion on effective marketing campaigns. He told us he sent it to 100 people, and he spent $25 for each video plus another $20 per person to mail it overnight. That is $45 per person, or $4,500 total for 100 people, just to mail the offer. 25 of those people chose the introductory offer for $1,000. So his initial investment, which seemed really high at $45 per mail piece, seemed like chump-change when you consider he made $25,000 from it. Of the 25 people who attended, 15 of them agreed to the $10,000 price he was charging for the annual membership. That was another $150,000 in sales that all came from the initial campaign.

What made this work so well was the initial list was super-targeted. These were all hand-chosen people he knew would be interested in this type of thing. The profit for each sale was high enough that it was easy to justify spending $45 per prospect just to put the offer in front of them.

In this case, he probably could not have made a better choice to market this particular product. The impact the video made was so impressive, I just couldn't help but want to be part of this group. Had he simply sent a flat letter, it would not have been nearly as impressive. That's what Lumpy Mail can do for you. It is one of the most powerful marketing strategies you can use.

But it is not right for every situation. Lumpy Mail is much more effective when you have a very specific target audience, and you know your product can fulfill their need. In addition, your sales price has to be high enough to justify the cost of the Lumpy Mail.

Do you have a list of properties that might justify doing something this outrageous? If so, you would be amazed at the results it could produce. Or maybe you can use a Lumpy Mail piece as a follow-up to those who respond to really get their attention.

WHAT IS THE BEST TYPE OF MAIL PIECE TO USE?

There is no right answer for this question. The best type of mail piece depends on what you're trying to do in your sales process. In many cases, using multiple different mail pieces is an effective strategy. Each mail piece has pluses and minuses given the situation. It's vital that you understand what you're doing, and how each type of mail piece could be used to get the best possible outcome.

I would like to point out some of the pros and cons of each of the five main types of mail pieces I have discussed.

In the real estate investor world, the most successful marketers use multiple types of mailers. The reason is that different prospects respond to different things. Remember earlier, I mentioned that one group of prospects that is attractive to most real estate investors is older people who have lived in their house for a long time, and own the home free and clear. We know that this group of people tends to be more traditional, and responds to things that are personalized. Both handwritten yellow letters, and business letters that look personalized do well with this group.

However, there are other people who are always in a hurry, sort the mail over the trashcan, and only give any mail piece a few seconds of their time. That type of person might respond better to postcards because they can see the message very clearly without opening an envelope.

Because there are all types of people in this world, and timing is always an issue, hitting someone multiple times, with multiple different mail pieces gives you the best chance of getting the most people's attention. A typical campaign might look like this:

Mailer #1: Small gcPowerMail Postcard (has Street View image plus text response option)

Mailer #2: Small "2ⁿᵈ Notice" Postcard

Mailer #3: Handwritten Yellow Letter

Mailer #4: Business Letter

Mailer #5: Handwritten Invitation Style Note

Mailer #6: Oversized gcPowerMail Postcard (has Street View image plus text response option)

You might also send a Lumpy Mail follow-up mailer to anyone who responds and sounds like a good prospect.

Remember, frequency is extremely important!

Chapter 10

Sales Copy Can Make or Break You

"Always enter the conversation already occurring in the customer's mind."
— Dan S. Kennedy, *The Ultimate Sales Letter*

Having effective sales copy is the third most important thing to success in any type of marketing, only preceded by going after the right target market, and getting the mail opened.

In direct mail marketing, copy tends to be more important than format or design. Don't get me wrong; effective formatting and design can accent the copy and help get your point across, but the copy itself is the most important thing. I'll give you some general rules for copywriting, and also talk specifically about different mail pieces and nuances of those mail pieces.

Probably the single most important thing you need to do when writing copy is to put yourself in the position of the person receiving your offer, and ask this question after every statement: "Who cares?" The "who" is the prospect. If the prospect doesn't care about every single thing you say in your copy, don't say it. This is true of headlines, sub-headlines, body copy, offers, guarantees, and bonuses. When you write, you always have to be thinking in terms of benefits to the person reading it. You want to make the benefits so compelling that they just have to respond to your offer.

POSTCARD COPY TIPS

In real estate, postcards are used as lead generation tools. There's just not enough space in a postcard to tell a complete sales story in most cases. Because of this, you have to be very concise and compelling to get the person to respond.

THREE RULES FOR POSTCARDS

1. Offer on front and back

When your prospect goes through their stack of mail, you have no control over which side of the postcard is up when they go through the stack. Remember, you only have three seconds to get their attention, and chances are they're only going to look at the side that is showing when they pick it up. It is vital to have your main offer and headline on both sides of the postcard, so that no matter what side they see they will get the main message.

2. Deadline on front and back

Another key element of effective copywriting is to have a deadline for their response. For the same reasons I just mentioned, having the deadline on both sides is critical.

3. Personalize front and back

It's a proven fact that the more you personalize a mailing, the more effective it is. Again, use their name and any other personalization you can add on both sides to give you the best possible chance to get their attention.

SALES LETTER COPY TIPS

Sales letters are typically contained in some sort of envelope. The envelope can be a regular business envelope, an invitation style envelope, a large priority mail type of

envelope, or some sort of Lumpy Mail packaging. In all cases, the job of the envelope is just to get someone to read the sales letter. The rest of this chapter is going to focus mainly on writing copy for sales letters. However, the same practices can be used for any sort of marketing, including postcards, print ads, and online marketing. Over the years, there have been many very successful campaigns that used a long sales letter in a newspaper or magazine.

Before I get into the details, I can already anticipate what you're going to say. You're going to say "Sales letters are too long. No one will read them." There is only one fact that matters in copywriting. It's not the length that matters. It's how interesting your copy is. If it's boring, you will lose the reader very quickly. But if it's compelling, they will read as long as it stays compelling, no matter how many pages that is.

In the real estate world, I will admit that almost all of the mailers we do are very short. Yellow letters are the shortest, typically consisting of only a couple of sentences. These mailers do work. However, if you want to stand out from your competition, and you have something to say as to why you stand out from your competition, writing a longer letter might make a lot of sense in your case. We have seen 8-page handwritten sales letters do well. What you're about to read is a basic lesson on sales letter copywriting. You can shorten it as much is you want if that's what you prefer.

BASIC ROADMAP OF GOOD SALES COPY

Below is a very rough outline of the basic components of a sales letter. These don't necessarily have to be in this exact order, but it should be close. There are some nuances. For instance, you can talk about the guarantee in many different places, including the headline. The earlier you talk about it the better.

Headline

Opening paragraph with benefits to reader - no more than three benefits

Credibility points

Lifestyle connection

Tell your story

Lay out pain points to reader

Tell more stories

Make irresistible offer - solve pain problem with benefits

Bonuses

Guarantee (can be anywhere)

Deadlines and scarcity

Testimonials (can use throughout)

Call to action

Close and signature

P.S.

P.P.S.

P.P.P.S. (The more the better!)

HEADLINE

The headline is the most important part of the copy. A good headline will get you 80% of the way to a response. The chief job of the headline is to get the reader to read the rest of the copy. You have to draw them in with the headline.

Headlines answer the following questions:

So what?	**What's in it for me?**
Who cares?	**Why are you bothering me?**

You need to spend a lot of time coming up with the ideal headline. A good way to do it is to brainstorm 50 to 100 different versions. Headlines are a fairly formulaic process. If you research people who are using effective headlines, you can sort of get an idea as to what is effective and what is not. Don't hesitate to swipe other headlines and make minor changes that apply to your market. After you've brainstormed your list, go through it and decide which ones you think are best. Often your second and third choices can become the sub-headlines under your main headline.

Use the Dan Kennedy guide to test your headline.

Will it make the reader read the next sentence?

Will it stand alone? (If you ran the headline and just a phone number in an ad, would you get a response?)

EXAMPLES OF EXCELLENT HEADLINES IN THE REAL ESTATE WORLD

Attention: I am buying houses in your neighborhood.

Bob, I want to buy your house.

Bob, I am interested in your home at 123 Main St.

Houses Wanted

I will buy 50 houses this year, and your house is on my list.

Have you recently inherited a house and would like to sell it fast with zero hassles?

Thinking of retiring and would like to sell your house without having to worry about fixing it up?

Notice

Second notice

Final notice

OPENING PARAGRAPH

Once you've written your headline and sub-headlines, the next stage is the opening paragraph. One huge mistake most people make is to immediately start talking about themselves in the opening paragraph. They start saying things like, "We have been in business for 50 years and we are located in a nice building..." Bad move.

You need to think back to what I said earlier about speaking the language of benefits to the prospect. Don't talk about yourself; talk about the prospect. Remember to ask the question, "Who cares?" after each line. The person who needs to care is the prospect.

You need to immediately start off with a benefit statement.

A good formula to use to help you with this process is the "if...then" formula. Using this formula will force you to start talking in terms of what will benefit the prospect. For example, "If you want to be extremely successful in your marketing, using the tips and techniques in this book will get you well on your way."

It is vitally important to remind the prospect why it is important for them to keep reading in the opening paragraph. Restate up to three benefits in the opening paragraph. No more than three.

CREDIBILITY POINTS

The next stage of effective copy is to establish your credibility. You need to prove to the prospect that you are worth listening to. Again, it's not about how long you've been in business and how nice your building is. It's about giving them a few key points to let them know you really do know what you're talking about. Tell them why being in business a long time matters to the prospect. You might say: "Our 23 years in the real estate industry give us the unique knowledge we need to solve any and every issue you may have."

ESTABLISH A LIFESTYLE CONNECTION AND PERSONALITY

Use social proof to talk about your lifestyle. Don't overtly talk about your success. Instead, say something like, "I jumped on the plane with my son to go see the Super Bowl last week." It implies that you are successful and have a lot of money without outright saying it. Most people can relate to wanting to spend time with their family. It is important because it adds further reasons for a person to listen to you.

TELL YOUR STORY

Telling a personal story about yourself is critical to successful bonding with the prospect. This may seem like it is in direct conflict with what I just said a minute ago about not talking about yourself. No one cares about the boring stuff that every business seems to talk about—good employees, good prices, nice building, etc. Telling a good story about yourself, designed to draw the reader in, is a good strategy. You need to put everything in terms that relate to the prospect.

An effective model for this is what we call the "hero's journey" model. Many movies follow this model with great success. You can use it in marketing as well.

Hero stories start out with the hero facing a problem, and enduring pain and hardship. Then the hero finds the answer to the problem, and with great sacrifice, ends up winning in the end, and living happily ever after. We can use that same model in our sales letters.

You start out talking about the hardship you had in the past. Focus a lot on the hardship and pain, especially those items that you know will relate to your prospects. Then you talk about the miracle breakthrough—the day you turned your life around.

Example:

> I was driving in my car home from a job I hated. I was sweating like crazy after a crappy day at work. I had the windows down because it was hot out and I couldn't afford to fix my air conditioning. I missed my kids' sporting events because I worked so much. I hated my life.
>
> Then I came across a marketing system that would teach me to start my own business. I didn't even have enough money to buy the system. But I knew that successful people invested in themselves, and I wanted to be successful. So I used the last few hundred dollars of credit I had on my credit card to buy the system. Using that system completely turned my life around. Today I work out of my house on the beach. I don't miss any of my kids' games. I vacation in tropical places, have a great relationship with my wife and I'm happier than ever.

It is vital that the story relates to what you really do for your customers. If they can relate to your story, the obvious solution is to purchase your product. Here is another version that speaks to a property owner you may be wanting to purchase from.

I know all about having a "less than ideal" house to sell. My mother passed away and my brother and I inherited her house. She had lived there for 40 years. The house needed a lot of work plus it had decades of clutter. Every time I started thinking about it, I stressed out.

I received a letter in the mail one day from a guy who said he could buy the house for cash "as is" and he could close fast. He even said that he would allow me to leave all the junk that I didn't want to clean out. He offered to do everything. At first his price offer seemed low, but then I started adding up the numbers.

It was going to take me at least 10 days of work just to clean up the house enough to be able to see what work needed to be done. That was 10 days I didn't have. Then I estimated the house had at least $25,000 of work needed to bring it in to decent condition to sell. Plus I had to pay a real estate commission and then even after it sold, I would be dealing with inspections. We all know that the inspectors always find stuff on old houses. It would probably be a 6-month project to get this done.

When I added it up, I would actually be making more money from the all-cash offer than I would have made had I sold the house through a real estate agent. Plus I didn't have to do all the work.

I did the deal and it was the best move I could have made. It went so well, I got interested in doing what the investor did and I ended up getting into the real estate business myself. Today I buy more than 25 houses a year – helping people just like me to get through that tough time. I can help you!

It is important to get the prospect to relate to you as a person. You need them to relate to your pain and suffering. They have it too. Think about the objections your customers might have when you're telling your story. Answer those objections as you tell the story.

KEY POINT: COPY MUST BE ENTERTAINING. IF YOU BORE PEOPLE, YOU LOSE THEM.

LAY OUT PAIN POINTS

After you've told your story, which should contain a lot of pain, you can clearly lay out the pain points in summary fashion for the reader. Later you're going to solve those pain points. You want to get him or her thinking about it.

TELL MORE STORIES

There is no better way to keep your copy entertaining and to illustrate points than to tell stories. Tell a story to illustrate each key benefit, pain point, and objection. The more stories you tell, the more you connect with the reader. Again, make sure to focus on pain and then solve the problem.

LAY OUT IRRESISTIBLE OFFER IN DETAIL

Here is where you lay it all out in a logical fashion for the reader to understand exactly what they're going to get. It must be in great detail, and focus on benefits to the reader. If you can monetize those benefits, it is even better. In other words, tell them the value of each service. Use the full retail value when you're doing this. The higher the number, the better. Then, at the end, give them an overall package price that is far cheaper than the individual items.

BONUSES

Always use bonuses. It is proven that adding bonuses increases response rates.

A bonus is exactly what you might think it is. It is something extra that you give the person when they respond. A rule of thumb is the more bonuses, the better. It is not uncommon for the list of bonuses to be longer than the list of benefits from the main offer. Make sure you monetize the bonuses as well. The larger the numbers, the better. We all like to get things for free, even wealthy people.

Free reports are the most common bonuses you see, especially in information marketing. Think about all the things you do for your customers, and if possible, package up some of those benefits into bonus packages.

84

Another effective strategy is to add a list of bonus choices that the prospect can choose from. This changes the thinking from *Yes or No* to *Which bonus do I want?*

ALWAYS USE GUARANTEES

Any guarantee is extremely important to removing risk in the mind of the prospect. If you can't guarantee 100% satisfaction, figure out what you can guarantee and list it.

If you can't guarantee what you sell, find something else to sell! Everyone can find a way to guarantee something. Don't be afraid of guarantees.

Many people are afraid to give 100% satisfaction guarantees because they are afraid dishonest people will take advantage of them. Yes, occasionally there is a dishonest person who's looking to get something for nothing and will try to take advantage of you. That is a fact of life. However, that is a small percentage, and a very small price to pay for the dramatic increase in sales you'll get by guaranteeing your product or services.

Three main types of guarantees

Satisfaction - If you're not satisfied we will give you back your money.

Results - If you don't get a certain result with the product or service we sell to you, we will give you back your money.

Perception - This is something that enhances the positive perception of you and your offer. "We promise to answer the phone with a smile on our face" is a perception guarantee.

More guarantees are better. When displaying a guarantee, make a big deal about it in your marketing materials. Put a box around it and make it look special. Do not bury it in the end; show it right up front. Including the guarantee in the headline is also a good strategy.

Guarantee in headline

"I will sell your house in 90 days or I'll buy it, guaranteed!"

Name your guarantees

Just like naming your offers, naming a guarantee will make it more memorable. The examples below are from copywriting guru Bill Glaser.

My personal, make you happy guarantee

I guarantee that selling your house to me will be the easiest, most pleasant transaction you've ever experienced. You will be so happy that you will have to pinch yourself to see if it's real.

My personal, super strength guarantee

I guarantee that this will be the biggest, baddest, most valuable seminar ever having to do with selling a house.

DEADLINES AND SCARCITY ARE CRITICAL

There is no offer without a deadline. People are famous for procrastinating. Even good intentions will often get lost at the bottom of the pile if there is not a deadline.

Plus, the deadline builds up the importance of the offer. If it is so great, there should be a limited supply. The deadline helps to promote the limited supply.

TESTIMONIALS

Testimonials are perhaps the most powerful tool you have in your arsenal. What other people say about you is much more believable than what you say about yourself. You need to use testimonials as much as you possibly can. You can never have too many.

Written testimonials are good. Audio or video testimonials are even better.

You can use them at any point in the sales copy. They can be part of the headline, interspersed in callout boxes, on the back of the sales letter, or on a completely separate sheet.

There are two major kinds of testimonials:

Outcome-driven Testimonial ....

What is the outcome the person got from using your product or service?

> Example:
>
> **"I received a 3% response for my mailings and was able to close 2 deals, which earned me $35,000 in profit. This is the best thing I have ever done!"**

Overcoming Objections Testimonial ·····················

These types of testimonials answer the objections that your typical prospects have. The best way to do this is to make a list of all the reasons people don't buy from you, then find testimonials that answer those objections.

"I had a million reasons why I was not going to buy from Joe. It seemed like he was lowballing me. But when he sat down and showed me that I was actually getting more net money from him than I would get by selling through an agent after all expenses and commissions, it turned out to be a great deal!"

One technique you can use to get testimonials written exactly the way you want them is to write them yourself, and get your customers to approve them. You will find that almost 100% of the time the customers will approve exactly what you've written. Of course this assumes they like you, so obviously you need to go to your best customers to utilize the strategy.

Don't use blind testimonials

Don't use partial names. The more information you can put about the person giving the testimonial, the better. Your goal is to prove it is from a real person.

Asking for testimonials is a normal course of business. When you do something good for someone and you know they're happy, ask them to take a moment and write that down and send it to you.

Contests are another good way to get testimonials. Send out a letter or email to all your clients, and ask them for testimonials in exchange for some reward. You can enter them all into a drawing for a prize of some sort. You'll be amazed at how easy it is to get people to respond to this.

Always get permission to use the testimonials. The best way to do this is at the time you're asking for the testimonial. People never say no, but it's still a good idea to ask.

Don't use the word "testimonials" in your marketing. Use words like "What clients say about us," or "What people have to say."

CALL TO ACTION

So many people miss this point when they create their marketing materials. They will list their contact information, but they don't specifically say what they want the reader to do. Spell it out in detail. It may sound dumb, but if you don't tell the reader exactly what to do, they often will not do anything, even if they are interested.

Call 800-xxx-xxxx within 48 hours!

Go to our webpage at www.callme.com and register today for your free gift.

CLOSE AND SIGNATURE

It may not seem like a big deal, but if this is a personal letter, you need to sign it like you are signing a personal letter. Use your full name and signature. If you are going for the true personal letter look, it is a good idea to sign in blue ink.

THE P.S.

The P.S. is the second most read part of a sales letter online or offline.

Why? Because people have been trained to know that all of the goodies are in the P.S.

The P.S. needs to include at least one of the following:

Restatement of the benefits	Indicate urgency or a deadline
Introduce a new benefit	Restate the guarantee
Restate the promise	Expand on the guarantee
Introduce a new promise	Restate the bonuses
Provide credibility	Restate the discounts

The more the better.

OTHER TIPS

NAME YOUR OFFER

An offer is more effective and memorable if it has a name. Something like the "Highest Price Home Sale Program" is more memorable than just "I will buy your house."

CREATE A "HATE" LIST

When writing copy, create a list of things the prospect hates, and then answer those objections.

BUILD VALUE

Break down your offer into parts. Show the value of each portion of the offer so it collectively sounds like a lot more than just one statement.

GIVE PAYMENT OPTIONS

Adding payment options will typically increase response. Allow the clients to make multiple payments over time, or offer a cash discount if they pay up front.

APPLES TO ORANGES COMPARISON

Always compare your offer to something else in order to build value. An example for a real estate business might be something like: "If you were to get a professional appraisal, it would cost you between $300 and $500. I will give you a market evaluation, FREE."

Add a deluxe offer to your choices. Typically, at least 20% of the people will choose a deluxe offer.

COPY LENGTH

The single most asked question in the copywriting business is "What is better, long copy or short copy?" People tend to think that if it's too long, no one will read it, especially in our fast-paced cell phone and Internet society.

It's not the length of the sales letter that determines whether or not they will read it. What matters is if they are interested in what you have to say. **If you bore them, they absolutely will not read it!**

If someone is interested in what you've got, they will read it forever.

The key is to find the right person, who has the best chance of being interested, and draw that person in with compelling headlines and a very interesting copy.

DUAL READERSHIP PATH

A dual readership path describes a method of writing that will allow you to reach different types of readers.

There are four main types of readers.

Scan-Man or Lady-Scan: Will scan only the headlines and never go back and read the details.

Detail Dude or Detail Darla: Will read the details top to bottom, headlines and all.

Mr. or Ms. Efficient: Will scan the headlines first, and if they're interested, read the details.

Timmy or Tina Trash: Won't read anything and is quick to use the round file.

When you use a dual readership path, you will highlight headlines, bullet points and callouts. The reader should be able to understand the offer after reading only those items.

By writing in this manner, you have a chance to grab the attention of Scan Man, Lady Scan, or Mr. or Ms. Efficient. Detail Dude and Detail Darla will read everything anyway, so you get them as well. There's nothing you can do for Timmy or Tina Trash, so don't worry about them.

Even the detail people sometimes scan first. It is almost human nature to quickly scan material to see if it holds our interest. If you write effectively, you can grab most people's attention during that scan.

GRAPHIC/COSMETIC ENHANCEMENTS

Graphic/cosmetic enhancements are almost as important as the copy itself. They will increase the likelihood of readership, and help guide the reader to the important points. I mentioned earlier you have to be interesting. Cosmetic enhancements help to make things interesting.

   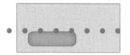

BENEFITS OF COSMETIC ENHANCEMENTS

Keep the person reading

Highlight the key points

Make long copy seem less intimidating

Relay your message by just reading the cosmetic information (dual readership path)

TYPES OF GRAPHIC/COSMETIC ENHANCEMENTS

Boldface	Subheads	Cross-outs
Underlining	Screens	Highlighting
Large fonts	Shading	Sidebars
Indenting	Handwritten notes	

What I'm not saying is to turn it into a graphic design masterpiece. Cosmetic enhancements are one thing. Turning it into nothing but a bunch of images, photos and graphics will often distract from the message.

Often when you turn a sales letter over to a graphic designer, they will turn an effective piece into a piece that doesn't pull at all. They get hung up on the graphics and minimize the importance of the words.

The main thing is you are trying to get a person to read your copy and get the message you're trying to send. If your graphic enhancements take away from that, they are not going to help. Use them, but don't overdo it.

Perhaps you didn't see my recent correspondence...

==Time is Running Out== on my Offer to BUY YOUR HOUSE FOR <u>CASH</u>

Dear «FULLNAME»,

I recently sent you an offer in the form of a check to buy the property you own at «PROPADD», «PROPCITY», «PROPST» «PROPZIP». I was not kidding when I sent that. It was a serious offer and time is running out for you to accept.

When I make an offer, I set aside funds to cover it. But I cannot keep those funds tied up indefinitely. If you don't say yes in the next week, I will reallocate that money to another property.

Let me just take a few minutes to explain why it makes sense to do business with us.

Target Real Estate Solutions is known as the premier Real Estate Investment company serving Ada and Canyon County. We pay cash, close quickly and structure SOLUTIONS for property owners. We work with the end in mind, creating WIN-WIN-WIN results.

We help home sellers, like yourself, benefit from ZERO commissions paid to Realtors, no repairs, decreased closing costs, an easy transaction with QUICK money in your hand. We strive to make this process as simple and seamless for all.

Simply call today for a guaranteed offer in 72 hours or less. I'll be glad to personally tell you more about my company and how we can work together. All calls are completely confidential and there is no obligation whatsoever.

Even if you are not interested in selling at this time, call ==«PHONE»==, so I can help you with determining the value of your property. Be sure to KEEP THIS LETTER. Thank you for your time and consideration and I look forward to speaking with you.

** Target Real Estate Solutions is *not* a real estate brokerage soliciting for listings**

Sincerely,

CALL ME!

Jeff Charlton
Target Real Estate Solutions

«PHONE»

No Hassle Guarantee

I guarantee that the purchase of your house will go exactly as I have laid out or I will write you a $1000 check.

P.S. The clock is ticking on this offer. If I don't hear from you within 5 business days from receipt of this letter, I will reallocate the finds I had set aside to purchase your property to another.

BIGGEST MISTAKES IN COPYWRITING

- Leaving out personal story

- No USP or good headline

- No guarantees or guarantee not up front

- No testimonials

- Looks and sounds boring

- No call to action

It is important to focus on the prospect or customer for the key elements of any marketing material. The key elements are the headline, the offer, the call to action, the benefits, the guarantees, and the postscript (P.S.).

But in between, you need to develop compelling copy that draws the reader in, establishes credibility, and enhances their chance of saying yes to your offer. Your goal is to connect you to the reader in a way that makes him or her relate to you as a human being. You want your readers to feel you are walking in their shoes. Stories make you credible. They establish you as a resource they should respect and want to do business with.

I want to spend a little bit more time on the personal story, because that is probably the single biggest mistake people make.

Why is a story important? Because that's how we are raised. Growing up, our parents read us stories. Our society likes stories.

The challenge is to work in the story at the right time. You should tell your story in every sales letter you write. And by the way, make sure it is a compelling story. Don't tell them your entire life story and all the boring details. Focus on the items that build interest in the product you sell and relate to the reader. Use the "hero story" format discussed earlier.

For instance, as a real estate investor, you might say something like:

> I grew up poor and had no money. I attended my first real estate seminar when I was 23 years old and in debt up to my ears. At the end of that weekend I thought my head was going to explode with all the information and I wasn't sure where to start. I was scared to death. So I went back to the beginning, and step-by-step did exactly what I was taught.
>
> Fast-forward to 10 years later.
>
> I still use some of those early techniques I learned at that seminar, and I have built a real estate empire of over 100 properties in my portfolio. We flip 15 properties every single month. I have reached a lifestyle beyond my wildest dreams. I spend more time with my children and wife, take more vacations, and have a larger bank account than I ever dreamed possible.
>
> I've taken everything I've learned over the last 10 years and packaged it up in this one super program. I'm going to teach you how to do exactly what I did and achieve the same success.

That is a story that a potential real estate investor would be interested in hearing. It establishes interest, credibility, and lets the reader know they are just like you. You'll notice at the beginning of this book I told my story. Hopefully it helped you to realize that you too can be successful in marketing if you just put your mind to it. If I can do it, anyone can do it.

Once you have a story, tell it every time. Use it in all your marketing materials where space permits. That doesn't mean it has to be in every single piece, but it should appear at least once as part of the sales process.

Effective marketing is all about effective communication and getting inside the head of the readers to motivate them to do what you want them to do. And you want them to feel good about doing it.

Chapter 11

Systems Key to Success

Scaling your business is all about processes and systems.

SYSTEMS + SYSTEMS + SYSTEMS = SUCCESS

At this point, you might be thinking to yourself that this sounds great, but it also sounds overwhelming. The way to overcome that feeling is to systemize everything.

THESE ARE THE THINGS YOU SHOULD HAVE IN PLACE

- Systems to identify potential prospects.

- Systems to make sure you collect information on all your prospects and customers so you can properly follow up.

- A database where you can store and easily retrieve that information.

- An email system that allows you to automatically send out messages to both prospects and customers.

- Separate marketing systems to handle prospects and customers (they should not be approached the same way).

- Systems to remind yourself to do regular marketing.

- Systems to ensure that regular marketing goes out on time each month.

- Systems in place so that all of your employees know exactly what to do, and when key employees are gone, other employees can step in and make sure the work gets done properly.

- Systems to make sure the customers feel important every time they contact your company.

Every one of these systems is vital to the success of your marketing program. If you don't have a system, you'll inevitably drop the ball, which will ultimately cost you money. You may not see it right away, but I guarantee you'll hurt yourself when you try to fly by the seat of your pants.

For a marketing system to be successful it has to be regular and predictable. To be predictable, mailings and advertisements have to go out on a regular basis, and you have to know what type of results you can expect from each of your campaigns in advance. The best way to know this is to have systems to make sure things get out on time, systems to track results, and systems to follow up and make changes.

Chapter 12

What Not to Do

Don't get hung up on things that don't matter to your success.

If you've gotten this far in the book, you've learned that there are a lot of key elements that are very important to success in marketing. But there also some elements that just don't matter. We see people getting hung up on insignificant things all the time— so much so that it gets in the way of their success. Here is a short list of things that are not important.

THICKNESS AND GLOSSINESS OF THE POSTCARD

A lot of postcard printing companies make a big deal about how thick their postcards are and how glossy and shiny they are. I can tell you that the thickness and the glossiness have zero impact on results. Yes your logo and personal photo may look nicer on a thick postcard, but people don't respond to offers because of thickness and glossiness. They

respond because the offer is compelling and they want to know more. Making something more glossy does not make it more compelling.

WEIGHT OF THE PAPER ON THE LETTER

This falls into the same category as above. A letter printed on 80 pound text is no more important than one printed on 60 pound text. In fact, in some cases a letter printed on what looks like a yellow legal pad, which is a fairly cheap paper, is more effective. It's counterintuitive, but in direct mail for real estate often the less professional, the better the response.

SPEED AT WHICH THE MAIL ARRIVES
(UNLESS THERE IS A TIME SENSITIVE EVENT INVOLVED)

This is another issue that often gets in the way of making good decisions. There is a huge difference in price between first-class mail and marketing mail. If done correctly, as described in this book, marketing mail can be just as effective as first-class mail. But it takes longer to get there. The only time speed matters, is if you have a specific date in mind for a specific event, and you waited to the last minute to do your mailing. Yes, in that case you had better use first-class mail to get it there as fast as possible.

In all other cases (with one possible exception when marketing to foreclosure or tax lien properties), especially if you are marketing every week or every month, whether it takes one week, two weeks, or four weeks for the mail to arrive is totally irrelevant. the only time it is relevant, is on your first mailing, if you are in a hurry to start seeing leads come through the door. In that case, yes, you might want to do your first mail drop first-class. But after that, you can do every other mailer marketing mail. You see, once you do your first mailing, you'll start getting a regular flow of leads. It doesn't matter to the prospect, or to you, how many weeks it took for the mail to go from the mail house to the prospect's mailbox. All that matters is that you get a steady flow of leads. Once the first batch comes in, as long as you are still mailing regularly, you will still get a steady flow of leads.

HOW MANY BAD ADDRESSES YOU GET BACK

Often, people mistakenly feel that the quality of a list is determined by how many non-deliverable returned mailers you get. Yes, a really old list may have a higher percentage of returned mail. But just because a list gets a large number of returned mail does not mean it's a bad list. What matters is return on investment, and that is all. If your mailing list is performing at a level that is profitable for you, then who cares how many returned envelopes you get? If it bothers you that much, and you are mailing to the same

list multiple times, then clean the list before you do your second mailing and you'll solve that problem.

Better yet, hire a skip tracing agency to track down the undeliverables, and go after those because they could be some of the hottest leads you will find.

COMMENTS FROM PEOPLE WHO ARE NOT POTENTIAL CLIENTS

Often when you do direct mail, you will get phone calls from people that complain for various reasons. They might complain that they don't want your junk mail because you're killing too many trees or something along those lines. If you're going after foreclosure properties, and you use a fairly aggressive tone, you might have people complaining because they are not in foreclosure. You can have people threaten to sue you for sending them direct mail. There are all kinds of crazy people in the world who get upset about all sorts of things. The reality is, if someone's going to take the time to call you and tell you how mad they are about you sending them mail, they were never a prospect in the first place. So don't worry about it. Smile, tell them thank you for their concern, and take them off the list for the next time. Or don't take them off the list. There are no laws against sending direct mail to anyone. You can't get sued for sending someone a piece of mail. So just don't worry about it. Spend your time worrying about the prospects that are viable and that you have a chance to turn into deals.

The bottom line in all this is do not get distracted from things that are not important to your long-term success. All the items above are simply distractions. Ignore them and focus on things that do matter.

Chapter 13

What Next?

*Make a plan and get off your butt
to go all in to execute it.*

The answer depends on where you are today.

If you are a beginning real estate investor, the best move you can make is to use proven systems and mailers, and don't try to reinvent the wheel. If you're a seasoned investor, and just want to upgrade your marketing program by adding direct mail, you too can use proven systems, or you can get into some of the more advanced strategies.

Since most of the people reading this report will be beginners, I'm going to focus on that group.

STEP 1: IDENTIFY YOUR MARKETING BUDGET.

If you want to be serious about success in real estate, you need to allocate a monthly marketing budget, and stick with it for at least a year. It's obvious that the more money you have for marketing, the faster you can go. However, even if you have limited resources, you need to identify a dollar amount that you are willing to spend no matter what, every single month for a year.

STEP 2: DECIDE IF YOU WILL DO IT YOURSELF, OR HIRE A PROFESSIONAL MAILING COMPANY.

Once you identify that amount, then you can back into just how much direct mail that will buy. If you don't mind doing some of the work yourself, you can go to your local copy store and have postcards or letters printed very inexpensively. This will get you the biggest bang for your buck, but will be very labor-intensive. The other drawback of doing it yourself is that the minute you get busy with trying to make deals, the marketing will fall by the wayside. It always does.

A much better strategy is to hire a professional direct mail marketing company, and lay out a long-term strategy. Lay out at least a three month plan, and then let the direct mail company handle it automatically. We at Graphic Connections Group do this every day for real estate investors all over the country.

STEP 3: IDENTIFY YOUR MAILING LIST.

No matter where you get your mailing list, I recommend that you take the time to go through the list to make sure the data is exactly what you want. I recommend that you export the leads into an Excel database, and go through them one by one to make sure that these are the exact prospects you want to target. You can then email that list to us manually, and we can set up your mailers from there. Doing this guarantees that your list will not have any errors or duplicates. Note: We can also remove duplicates for you if you don't want to mess with that step.

STEP 4: CHOOSE THE TYPE OF MAILER OR MAILERS YOU WANT TO USE.

Do you want to use postcards or letters? Handwritten or typed? Size? Type of paper? Postage type? Frequency? All these questions need to be answered. I would suggest using some of the standard programs that we have already identified to work.

STEP 5: GET A TRACKING PHONE NUMBER
SO YOU CAN TRACK RESULTS PER MAILER.

There are a bunch of companies online that can give you a tracking phone number that will allow you to track results from one mailer to the next. These systems are inexpensive and very simple to use. You may ask your mailing company if they have one. The idea is to use a different phone number for every mailer that you use so that you know how many responses come from each mailer. You could do this manually, but we have found that very few people are effective in doing this. Plus most call tracking systems will also record the phone calls and give you all sorts of other statistics that are valuable.

STEP 6: GET YOUR CONTACT AND RESPONSE INFORMATION
TO THE MAILING COMPANY.

Are you going to ask for the recipients to call you, email you, go to a website, or some other method of contact? Make sure you test all of your systems prior to dropping the mail to make sure everything is working properly.

STEP 7: INSIST ON PROOFS.

Never do any sort of direct mail piece without getting a proof of the final piece first. It's a good idea to ask for a proof that has been merged with your list to make sure that the merge fields appear properly as well. Most real estate lists have a property address and a property owner address. Make sure that those address fields appear in the proper place on your mailer, and that they are not mixed up.

STEP 8: SET YOUR MAIL SCHEDULE.

Lay out the schedule of mail drops, taking into consideration postal delivery times, and your ability to handle responses. If you're doing a large mailing, you might want to spread out the drops so that all of the calls don't come in at the same time.

STEP 9: PULL THE TRIGGER.

Once you approve the mail piece and everything is in order, pull the trigger and get the mail into the mail stream.

STEP 10: STAY THE COURSE.

No matter what your response rates are in the beginning, the worst thing you can do is quit. If you've done your job with a good list, and are using a proven mailer, you will get responses eventually. But they may not call right away, especially if you're doing a very small mailing. Many beginners only mail 250 to 500 pieces of mail. It is not unusual to only get a few calls from quantities that small. That doesn't mean you still can't be successful. We had a client who at one time mailed 100 pieces of mail, and she closed two houses. Yes!

Chapter 14

Advanced Strategies

*Don't try to reinvent the wheel. Find
someone who has already been where you
want to go and do what they did.*

If your business is not where you want it to be, you need to sit down and take a hard
look at it. The first thing you need to do is assess where you stand today. You can't move
forward until you know where you are. A completely comprehensive marketing system is
a large undertaking. You may already have part of the critical elements in place.

START WITH THE PERSONAL ASSESSMENT

Below is a checklist to use for this purpose. Once you assess where you are today, you can decide where to go from here.

☐ Do you have a steady flow of leads?

☐ Do you know exactly how much business you will do next week, next month, or next year?

☐ Do you have a plan to grow even when the economy is down?

☐ Do you want to grow?

☐ Do you have a system to replace the natural attrition that happens with every business?

☐ Do you have a website?

☐ Do you have a unique selling proposition (USP)?

☐ How do you introduce your product to new prospects?

☐ Do you have outside sales people?

☐ Do you have inside sales people?

☐ Are you a retail location?

☐ Does your product or service offer repeat business or one-time sales?

☐ Do you have existing customers?

☐ Do you have a database with information about all your existing customers?

☐ Have you identified your ideal customer, and their characteristics?

☐ How much revenue and profit comes from a typical sale?

☐ What is the lifetime value of a customer?

☐ How often do repeat customers order from you?

☐ Do you use any sort of advertising or direct response marketing now?

☐ Do you have existing sales copy already written?

☐ Do you have a marketing budget?

☐ Do you know how much it costs you in advertising and marketing to obtain a new customer?

☐ Do you have any experience in direct mail marketing or advertising?

- ☐ Are you a writer?

- ☐ Are you willing to learn how to write copy yourself? If not, are you willing to pay someone else to do it?

- ☐ Do you have a current prospect list with names addresses, phone numbers and emails?

- ☐ Do you guarantee your products?

- ☐ Do you have an auto-responder such as Constant Contact or AWeber?

- ☐ Do you have a CRM system such as Salesforce, or Infusionsoft?

- ☐ Do you publish a newsletter?

- ☐ Do you have a blog on your website? Do you post to it?

- ☐ Do you use social media in your marketing?

- ☐ Do you use radio, or TV, or print advertising?

- ☐ Do you have a system in place to track results from mailings and advertisements?

- ☐ Have you ever used online advertising such as pay-per click, banner ads, or re-marketing?

Once you've done the self-assessment, look at the elements you do not have in place and decide what you think will give you the biggest bang for your buck in the shortest possible time.

Then get to work.

If you basically know what you need to do, and just need help implementing a direct mail strategy, you can find a direct response marketing company who has the expertise in helping you craft your entire program, and work with them. My company, Graphic Connections Group, does just that. We can take you from where you are today to a completely comprehensive program, no matter how far away you are.

You may just need a few tweaks; you may need it all.

Give us a call today at 636-519-8320, or go to our website at www.REIprintmail.com, and click on the **Contact** button at the top of the page.

We would love to help you on your journey to marketing prominence in the real estate industry.

Chapter 15

Bonus Ideas

This last section is just a compilation of a bunch of miscellaneous ideas that might help you. Enjoy!

SHOULD I MAIL DURING THE 4TH QUARTER HOLIDAYS?

Most marketers would say no. They would say that people are distracted by the holidays and that you're wasting your money on direct mail for real estate during this time. I disagree with one caveat.

If you are brand-new and have never mailed anything, I would wait until January 1 to start your brand-new marketing campaign, because people do get distracted during the holidays. It is a fact that there's a chance that the mail will get lost in the pile of holiday cards and tons of retail holiday special deals. You will get a lower response rate during the holidays than throughout the rest of the year in most cases.

So if you're brand-new, I would not start off during this difficult marketing season.

However if you are a seasoned marketer, and have already been marketing every month, then my advice is just the opposite. Keep mailing. The reason for this is that if you stop marketing in mid-November and don't do anything till the first of the year, you will have six weeks with no leads coming in. That means you're pretty much guaranteed to have a terrible November and December in terms of sales and profits.

Yes, your response rates may be a little less. But they won't be zero. There are some people that are still going to be interested in selling their house during this time. And if you've been marketing all year, you should have profits and cash flow to be able to fund a little higher cost on marketing during the fourth quarter.

There is one benefit to marketing during the month of December that most people don't think about. Because it is the generally accepted wisdom that you should not market during the fourth quarter, there will be less competition. So even though it may be harder to get the prospect's attention, because you will have fewer competitors, you still have a good chance of success if you follow the other principles outlined in this book.

**Remember, mail, mail, mail, and mail some more,
and watch your profits go up, up, up!**

THANKSGIVING CARD STRATEGY

If you are sending out holiday or Christmas cards during December, stop doing it. Not because I have anything against Christmas or the holidays. However, most companies send out cards during that time period, and because there are so many, your card could get lost in the shuffle.

Rather than do it at Christmas, why not send out a card at Thanksgiving? Thanksgiving is the time for giving thanks anyway, so it makes sense to thank your customers during that time. And very few people, if any, are sending cards at that time, so yours will get noticed. It is an excellent goodwill gesture.

Kick it up a notch: In addition to sending the Thanksgiving card, put a sealed envelope inside the card that says on the outside, "Please open this only after you finish displaying your Thanksgiving card."

People's natural curiosity will get them to open that envelope right away to see what's in it. Put some sort of an offer inside that envelope.

USE SWIPE FILES

A swipe file is a file you keep of examples of ads, sales letters, and marketing pieces from other people in all types of industries that you think are good. Simply save them in a file, and when it is time for you to create a marketing piece, refer to that file for ideas. There's no point in reinventing the wheel. Caution - do not blatantly plagiarize anything.

Using swipe files for ideas is great, but make sure you change them enough to make it original to you.

Keep rewriting copy of campaigns already written. If you have something that's working well, rewrite it slightly differently.

BORROW IDEAS FROM OTHER INDUSTRIES

Who's got stuff that's really working? It doesn't matter if it's not in your industry. If something is working in another industry, figure out how to use the same concept in your business, and deploy it.

TURN ADS INTO LETTERS, LETTERS INTO POSTCARDS

There is no need to continually reinvent the wheel. Once you have a marketing message, using that same message reformatted in different pieces is smart.

Q&A FORMAT FOR QUICK SALES LETTERS

One way to crank out a quick message is to use the Q&A format. Write down the top 6 to 10 questions you know your customers have, and then answer the questions. It's simple.

RECORD THE PRESENTATION OF SOMEONE WHO SELLS A PRODUCT OR SERVICE REALLY WELL

Find a top salesperson in your industry, and see if you can record one of their sales presentations. Use what they say in your copy. Since they are successful, you'll probably learn things you'll never hear anywhere else. They can be very powerful. If you are successful, then record your own presentation. You will learn things just hearing your own words and how you relate to clients that will work well in your marketing efforts.

DO JOINT VENTURE DEALS

One of the most powerful ways you can get introduced to potential customers is to find someone else you trust and respect who is selling a product to the same types of people who fit your ideal customer profile. Make a deal with them to market your products to each other's lists. Exactly how this deal is structured is up to your imagination.

Information marketers are especially adept at doing this. I will use me as an example, since I am primarily a direct mail guy. It would make sense for me to form a relationship

with a guy like Kent Clothier. He sells mailing list systems, training and consulting services. What we sell complements that. He directs clients to us. When we do a good job for his clients, it makes him look good. We both win. Don't be afraid to offer your partners some sort of revenue share to sweeten the pot. Always, always, do a great job!

SHARE LISTS – AFFILIATE MARKETING

Sharing lists and affiliate marketing are very similar to the previous section about joint venture deals. The only difference is how you handle it. Typically when you share lists, you might just make an agreement to trade your list with someone else and that's the end of it. It is still a good deal for two people in noncompeting but complementary markets.

Affiliate marketing typically involves giving an affiliate the link to your website, and they will market your products to their list, in a completely hands-off fashion. All they are doing is sending an email to their list, recommending you, and asking the recipients to click on a link which takes them to your website. That link has tracking codes in it so you can calculate your affiliate commission properly.

Affiliate marketing is an extremely powerful way to dramatically increase your sales almost overnight. If you can find a person who has a very large email list, you'll be amazed at what can happen with one email.

REFERRAL MARKETING

Referral marketing is probably one of the most effective ways that just about any business can increase sales without having a huge and complicated marketing system in place. It boils down to encouraging your customers to give you referrals at the time they are the happiest in your transaction. This usually occurs right after the sale is made.

There are a lot of different ways to do this, but the essence is to ask a person for a referral and reward them when they give you one. Make it easy for them to refer you by offering some sort of introductory offer to the person they're referring. People who are referring you want to look good in the eyes of the people they're talking to. By giving them a special deal to offer, it's going to make them look like they are doing their friends a favor.

An example might be to offer $1,000 cash to a referrer when the deal they referred closes. You can offer the referee a free move-out service that you don't offer otherwise. This way the referrer looks good to the referee, and they are especially happy when you hand them that check for $1,000. You had better believe they will be looking for someone else to refer to you.

Every single person who buys from you and has a good experience should be encouraged to give you referrals in a nonthreatening and easy way.

One very simple way is to include a shock and awe referral box with every order that is fulfilled. If the order is something you hand-deliver, you can hand-deliver the referral box as well. If your business involves you shipping orders to people, it's very simple to attach an additional box or envelope to the side of the same shipping container for almost no extra money.

DON'T LET YOUR LETTERS OR DESIGNS GET STAGNANT

When mailing to customers or prospects you have already spoken to, you need to mix things up a bit. Sending the same designs over and over to customers is fine for a while, but soon it will cause them to lose interest.

Your mailings should be attention-grabbing and informative, not stale and boring. If you recently started offering a new service, a postcard letting your database know about it would be a smart move. The main point is to keep your company in the front of their mind and to keep them reading your postcards.

If you send the same cards to your customer database and your customers lose interest, you are wasting your money on postage. Your postcards won't get the attention you want.

COLLECT ALL THE INFORMATION YOU CAN FROM YOUR CUSTOMERS AND PROSPECTS

It sounds like a no-brainer, but you would be surprised by how many companies fail to collect key client data. Names, addresses, phone numbers, emails, and even birthdays can be very useful.

It's not a bad idea to log the date they became a customer, and then use that in an anniversary mailing at some point in the future. Of course that's the anniversary of the day they became a customer, not their wedding anniversary.

SPELL YOUR CLIENTS' NAMES CORRECTLY

Getting people's names wrong is like punching them in the face. No one likes to see their name spelled incorrectly. Take the time to make sure you get this right.

DON'T TREAT YOUR CUSTOMERS LIKE PROSPECTS

While form letters and generic emails may be easier for you, don't make the costly mistake of treating your customers like prospects. Have different letters and email sequences for customers and prospects. Once a prospect has moved into the customer field, stop sending them prospect mail.

BECOME AN EXPERT IN YOUR FIELD - WRITE A BOOK

There is no quicker way to claim expert status on any topic than to write a book. There's something magical about putting ink on paper in the form of a written book. Our society has a high regard for authors; it doesn't seem to matter if the author actually knows what they're talking about or not.

Even if you are relatively new to a topic, all it takes is a little research, and putting things in your own words, and you can crank out a book in a very short time.

That may seem like an overwhelming task. I assure you, it can be done quickly. I'll let you in on a little secret. I wrote this book in about 30 total hours of my time.

How did I do that so quickly? First of all, it helps to actually be an expert. I have been studying marketing and direct mail for over 25 years. I know it backwards and forwards. So for me, all I had to do was create an outline of topics, then a few subtopics under each main topic, and I was ready to go. I didn't need to do any research, because I already knew enough to write something that makes sense and is helpful to the reader.

I then spoke into a microphone using voice recognition software, about each topic and subtopic.

I went through all the topics initially in about 8 hours. I then went back a second time and did some editing, and organized my thoughts. At that point, I added, subtracted and organized. That took another 8 hours or so of time.

I then passed the book onto an editor, and had that person do a rough edit, and rough proofread.

They gave me the book back, and I went through it again, page by page, editing it myself.

I handed it back to the editor a second time, then went through it one last time myself. Lastly, I turned it over to my graphic design department to make it look pretty. All totaled,

about 30 hours of my time, and about 3 calendar weeks allowing for some wasted time between steps.

TEST TEST TEST

This is the one area where many marketers fall down. They think that they know everything there is to know about their prospects, and how they think. They think they can write copy and then just roll it out without a test. I cannot stress enough, that no matter how much you think you know about your customer, and how much you think an offer is going to work, do not bet the farm on any campaign until you test it first.

For a test to be statistically valid, you need at least 5,000 pieces of mail. Unfortunately, a lot of marketers either cannot afford to mail 5,000, or don't have a list that is that large in total.

So my recommendation is whatever the size of your list, break it down into at least three parts. Mail to no more than one third of the list the first time around as a test. Then evaluate the results, and go from there. The exception is if your list is under 500 names. In that case, you really have no choice but to mail to the entire list and see what happens. Anything less is not a valid test anyway.

Once you establish a successful mail piece, keep using it until you're able to find another mail piece that is more successful. What that means is do side-by-side testing, pairing the successful piece against the new piece. If the new piece pulls better, it can then be your standard mailer. If it does not pull better, tweak it and try again. Never abandon a successful mail piece until you have something that is proven to pull better. Once you've established acceptable results from your primary mail piece, then you can mail to your entire list.

Chapter 16

Good is Good Enough

I have always been a ready fire aim kind of guy. You have enough information from this book to start your direct mail campaign tomorrow.

GO MAKE SOMETHING HAPPEN
AND THEN WORRY ABOUT HOW YOU GOT THERE LATER.

Marketing can be an overwhelming task. People can spend weeks, months, even years, trying to perfect a marketing campaign, thinking it has to be perfect before they release it. The problem is, it'll never be perfect. You don't know what works and doesn't work until you release it. So do your best the first time around, and get it out. You can make adjustments to it from there.

In this book you have been introduced to concepts that are proven to work in the real estate investment field. Don't try to reinvent the wheel. Pick some proven mailers and get them in the mail. Start driving some phone calls and see how things go. You can then adjust your marketing accordingly as you gain experience. You can switch mailers, lists, offers, etc. Marketing is not an exact science; it is always a moving target. You start with a control, which is your first mailer, and then you keep trying to improve on it from there.

There's a rule of thumb in marketing that if something is working, keep using it until it doesn't work. Although I agree with that, there's also something to be said for mixing it up a little to keep it fresh. You can keep the same basic ideas, headlines, and hooks that work, but change the designs a little bit so the people don't get accustomed to seeing the same thing over and over again and then just throw it away.

Take your best shot and go. Good is good enough.